Reflections

CALIFORNIA SERIES

The United States: MAKING A NEW NATION

Homework and Practice Book

Grade 5

Harcourt
SCHOOL PUBLISHERS

Orlando   Austin   New York   San Diego   Toronto   London

Visit The Learning Site!
www.harcourtschool.com

The activities in this book reinforce social studies concepts and skills in Harcourt School Publishers' *Reflections: The United States: Making a New Nation*. There is one activity for each lesson and skill. In addition to activities, this book also contains reproductions of the graphic organizers that appear in the chapter reviews in the Student Edition. Study guides for student reviews are also provided. Reproductions of the activities pages appear with answers in the Teacher Edition.

Contents

The Land and States

DIRECTIONS Read each list of three states. Use the map to find a fourth state that borders all three. Write the name of the state and its capital.

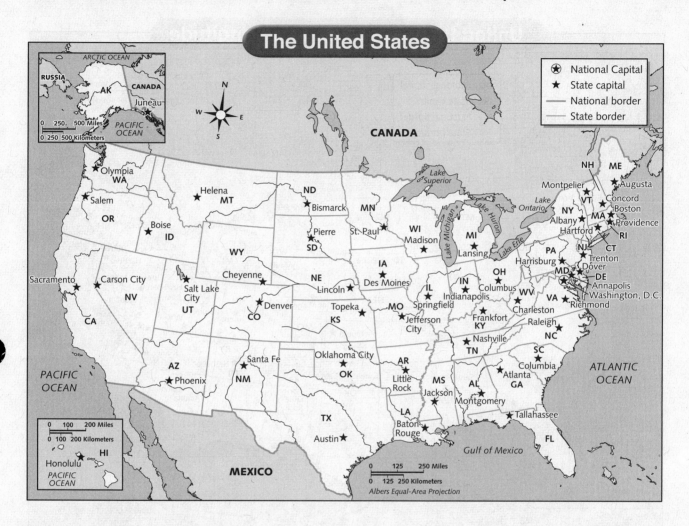

The United States

1. Massachusetts, Vermont, Maine _____ , _____

2. Indiana, Michigan, Pennsylvania _____ , _____

3. Mississippi, Florida, Georgia _____ , _____

4. Oregon, Nevada, Arizona _____ , _____

5. Arizona, Nevada, Idaho _____ , _____

CALIFORNIA STANDARDS HSS 5.9; CS 4

Name _____ Date _____

Skills: Use Latitude and Longitude

DIRECTIONS Use the map to find each latitude and longitude given below, and then write the name of the state in each location.

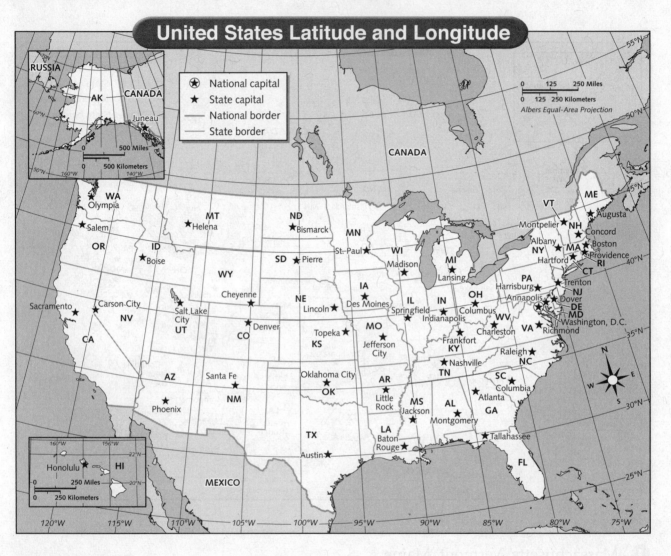

United States Latitude and Longitude

National capital
State capital
National border
State border

RUSSIA
CANADA
AK
Juneau

CANADA

MEXICO

WA
Olympia
Salem
OR
ID
Boise
MT
Helena
ND
Bismarck
MN
St. Paul
SD
Pierre
WY
Cheyenne
NE
Lincoln
IA
Des Moines
WI
Madison
MI
Lansing
Sacramento
Carson City
NV
CA
Salt Lake
City
UT
CO
Denver
Topeka
KS
MO
Jefferson
City
IL
Springfield
IN
Indianapolis
OH
Columbus
AZ
Santa Fe
NM
Phoenix
Oklahoma City
OK
AR
Little
Rock
MS
Jackson
AL
Montgomery
GA
LA
Baton
Rouge
TX
Austin
TN
Nashville
KY
Frankfort
WV
VA
Richmond
Charleston
NC
Raleigh
SC
Columbia
Atlanta
FL
Tallahassee
VT
Montpelier
NH
Concord
ME
Augusta
Albany
NY
MA
Boston
Hartford
CT
RI
Providence
PA
Harrisburg
NJ
Trenton
DE
Dover
MD
Washington, D.C.
Annapolis

HI
Honolulu

1. 30°N, 100°W _____

2. 40°N, 90°W _____

3. 40°N, 80°W _____

4. 40°N, 110°W _____

5. 30°N, 90°W _____

CALIFORNIA STANDARDS HSS 5.9; CS 4

(continued)

2 ■ Homework and Practice Book   Use after reading Chapter 1, Skill Lesson, pages 22–23.

© Harcourt

The Desert Southwest

DIRECTIONS Fill in the blanks in the sentences below, using terms from the Word Bank.

adapt	adobe	division of labor	staple	surplus

1 The American Indians of the desert Southwest had to _____ their lifeways to meet the challenges of the environment.

2 Maize, beans, and squash were the _____ foods of the Pueblo Indians.

3 Pueblo Indians built houses from _____, which could be made of clay mixed with straw.

4 Having a _____ of food meant survival to the people of the desert Southwest in times of drought.

5 The _____ in Hopi society meant that important jobs were divided between men and women.

© Harcourt

Name _____ Date _____

DIRECTIONS Read the facts listed below the chart. Then write the number of each fact in the correct column of the chart.

Hopi	Navajo

1 called themselves *Diné*, meaning "The People"

2 lived in pueblos

3 ancestors were the Ancient Puebloans

4 families often lived far from one another

5 lived in hogans

6 called their gods the Holy People

7 well known for their pottery making

8 taught other groups how to farm

9 used sandpaintings in ceremonies

10 lived in villages, usually led by a chief

DIRECTIONS Choose one of the groups shown on the chart above. Write a paragraph about the group and its customs on a separate sheet of paper. Use the chart to help you write your paragraph. You may also include facts that are not on the chart.

© Harcourt

Use after reading Chapter 2, Lesson 1, pages 52–58.

The Pacific Northwest

DIRECTIONS Use the Word Bank to identify the uses of the natural resources in the pictures below. A term may be used more than once.

homes	tools	boats	food	totem poles
water	fish	transportation	masks	oil for lamps

Trees

_____

_____

_____

_____

_____

_____

Whales

_____

_____

_____

Water

_____

_____

_____

CALIFORNIA STANDARDS HSS 5.1, 5.1.1, 5.1.2, 5.1.3

Name _____   Date _____

The Plains

DIRECTIONS Read the labels above the boxes. Draw a picture of each item.

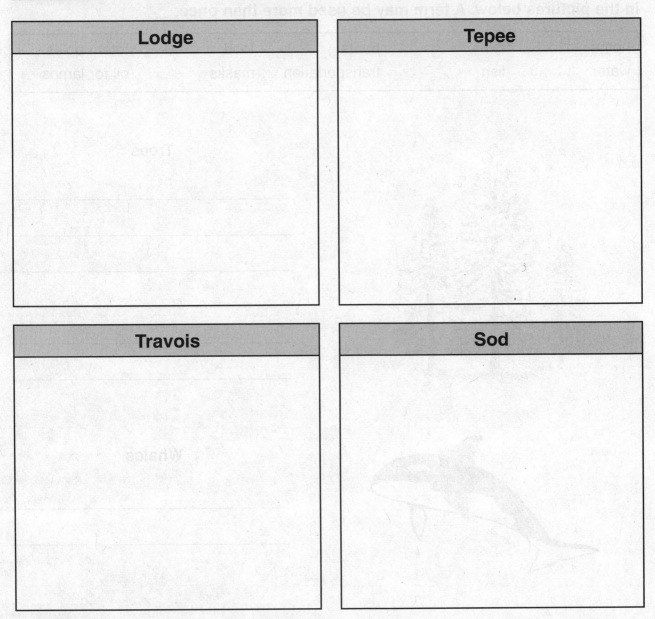

Lodge	Tepee

Travois	Sod

DIRECTIONS Choose one of the items you drew. Write a sentence or two describing how the item was made or used.

_____

_____

_____

CALIFORNIA STANDARDS HSS 5.1, 5.1.1; HI 2

Name _____ Date _____

The Eastern Woodlands

DIRECTIONS **Read the passage. Then answer the questions that follow.**

In the late 1500s, Iroquois villages often battled among themselves. Often, these battles grew out of small disputes. According to tradition, a Huron named Deganawida believed that the battles must stop if the Iroquois tribes were to protect their ways of life from European newcomers. Deganawida persuaded a Mohawk leader named Hiawatha to join him in spreading throughout Iroquois country the message that "All shall receive the Great Law and labor together for the welfare of man."

The result of their effort was a confederation called the Iroquois League, made up of the Five Nations of the Seneca, the Cayuga, the Onondaga, the Oneida, and the Mohawk. A few years later, a sixth nation, the Tuscarora, joined the league.

Each nation in the league governed itself, and matters were often settled by unanimous vote. Very important matters, such as war, were left for discussion by a Grand Council of 50 chiefs.

1 Who was Deganawida?

_____

_____

_____

2 Why did Deganawida think it was important to stop the fighting?

_____

_____

3 What tribes belonged to the Iroquois League?

_____

_____

4 How did the Iroquois League make decisions that affected all its nations?

_____

5 What do you think Deganawida meant when he said, "All shall receive the Great Law and labor together for the welfare of man"?

_____

_____

© Harcourt

 CALIFORNIA STANDARDS HSS 5.1, 5.1.3; HI 2

Name _____ Date _____

Skills: Resolve Conflict

DIRECTIONS Complete the graphic organizer below. For each step, write the decisions that led to the formation of the Iroquois League.

Identify the Problem
1 _____

⬇

All Sides Clearly State Wants and Needs
2 _____

⬇

All Sides Decide What is Most Important
3 _____

⬇

All Sides Plan and Discuss Possible Compromises
4 _____

⬇

All Sides Plan a Lasting Compromise
5 _____

© Harcourt

CALIFORNIA STANDARDS HSS 5.1, 5.1.3

The Arctic

DIRECTIONS Read each question below, and choose the best answer. Then fill in the circle for the answer you have chosen.

1 What did Arctic peoples most often use to build their homes?
  (A) stones   (C) adobe
  (B) wood   (D) ice

2 What did Arctic peoples most often use to make tools?
  (A) iron   (C) wood
  (B) bones   (D) stones

3 How did Arctic peoples get most of their food?
  (A) by hunting   (C) by trading
  (B) by farming   (D) by gathering

4 What did Arctic peoples use as fuel for fires?
  (A) wood   (C) seal blubber
  (B) sod   (D) buffalo chips

5 Which of the following was NOT hunted by Arctic peoples?
  (A) caribou   (C) seals
  (B) foxes   (D) buffalo

© Harcourt

CALIFORNIA STANDARDS HSS 5.1, 5.1.1

Skills: Use Tables to Group Information

DIRECTIONS Fill in the blanks to complete the table.

Table A: Tribes and Their Staple Foods		
Tribe	**Climate and Geography**	**Staple Foods**
Hopi	hot, dry desert	
Makah		salmon, whales
	dry, flat plains	
Iroquois	moderate climate, forest	
	extremely cold, harsh land	

![bear] **CALIFORNIA STANDARDS HSS 5.1, 5.1.1; HI 2**   *(continued)*

20 ▪ **Homework and Practice Book**   Use after reading Chapter 2, Skill Lesson, pages 88–89.

© Harcourt

Name _____ Date _____

Complete the table below. Use the information from the table on page 20, but group the information in a new way.

Table B: Staple Foods by Tribe		
Staple Foods	**Climate and Geography**	**Tribe**
_____ _____	hot, dry desert; moderate climate, forest	_____
_____	rainy coastal area	_____
_____	_____	_____
_____	_____	_____

DIRECTIONS Use the information in both tables to answer the questions below.

1 Which table makes it easier to find out what the climate is like where an

American Indian tribe lives? _____

2 What table would you use if you wanted to find out what staple foods can be

found in different climates? _____

3 Which table makes it easier to find out which staple foods American Indian

tribes had in common? _____

Use after reading Chapter 2, Skill Lesson, pages 88–89.

Study Guide

DIRECTIONS Fill in the missing information in these paragraphs about American Indians. Use the terms listed below to help you complete the paragraph for each lesson.

Lesson 1	Lesson 2	Lesson 3	Lesson 4	Lesson 5
surplus	bartered	council	confederation	kayaks
ceremonies	clan	tepees	Iroquois	harpoons
adobe	potlatch	sod	Algonquians	igloos

Lesson 1   The peoples of the desert Southwest had to adapt to a land with extreme temperatures and little water. They planted their crops at the bottoms of mesas, where they could catch rainwater. They used stones and mud or _____ to build pueblos. They stored _____ corn to eat when food was scarce. To bring good harvests, they held _____ that lasted several days.

Lesson 2   In the Pacific Northwest all the members of a _____ often lived together in a longhouse. The various groups in the region formed large trade networks. People _____ for goods at trading centers such as The Dalles. People from dozens of tribes, some speaking very different languages, traveled hundreds of miles to trade there. Wealthy people showed their wealth by giving a celebration called a _____. This celebration might last up to ten days and include dancing, food, and speeches.

© Harcourt

🐻 **CALIFORNIA STANDARDS HSS 5.1, 5.1.1, 5.1.2, 5.1.3**

(continued)

Use after reading Chapter 2, pages 52–89.

Name _____ Date _____

Lesson 3 Plains Indians had varied ways of life. In areas where grass was
plentiful, some people built lodges covered with _____. Other
groups used buffalo skins to make tents called _____. Among
the Lakota, each group governed itself. The Cheyenne leaders gathered as
a _____ to make decisions that all Cheyenne followed. The
buffalo was the main source of food for all the American Indian groups that
lived on the Great Plains.

Lesson 4 The _____ lived in the northeastern part of the
Eastern Woodlands, around the Great Lakes. They grew crops, and they also
hunted and fished. In the 1500s, they formed a _____ to settle
their disputes and to defend themselves. The _____ lived farther east, on the Coastal Plain. Because of the plentiful supply of fish near
the coast, these tribes relied less on growing crops.

Lesson 5 The peoples of the Arctic region adapted to a frozen, barren land.
At times, they used ice to build homes called _____. From animal skins, they made _____ that they paddled on the sea. They
used _____ to hunt seals and other animals that they depended
on to meet most of their needs. These ways helped the peoples of the Arctic
region adapt to and survive in harsh surroundings.

READING SOCIAL STUDIES: COMPARE AND CONTRAST

Focus Skill American Indians

DIRECTIONS Complete this graphic organizer to show that you can compare and contrast the American Indians who lived in different regions of North America.

Topic 1

Pacific Northwest People

used whales for food and oil; made totem poles

Similar

_____

_____

_____

_____

Topic 2

Eastern Woodlands People

some groups grew crops; used wampum

Topic 1

The Arctic People

_____

_____

_____

_____

_____

_____

Similar

They adapted their way of life to a harsh environment.

Topic 2

The People of the Desert Southwest

_____

_____

_____

_____

_____

© Harcourt

CALIFORNIA STANDARDS HSS 5.1, 5.1.1, 5.1.2, 5.1.3

Exploration and Technology

DIRECTIONS Fill in the missing words in this letter from Christopher Columbus to Queen Isabella. Use the terms in the Word Bank.

technology

expedition

benefits

empire

costs

Dear Queen Isabella,

Thank you for agreeing to pay for my _____. With an improved compass and astrolabe, I am sure that I have the _____ I need to reach Asia. As you know, the _____ of the journey are high. But I assure you, the _____ also will be great. Your _____ will gain great wealth and vast lands.

Your servant,

Christopher Columbus

© Harcourt

A Changing World

DIRECTIONS Read each statement about the aims, obstacles, and accomplishments of the explorers listed below. In the space provided, write the name of the explorer who would have been most likely to have made the statement.

Balboa	Caboto	Magellan	Vespucci

1. "I sailed to a place south of where Columbus had landed, but the coast I traveled along did not match Polo's descriptions of Asia." _____

2. "I led the first European expedition to reach the Pacific Ocean."

   _____

3. "It took us more than three months to cross the Pacific Ocean, and many among my crew died of hunger and illness." _____

4. "The English king sent me on an expedition to the Indies, to help England compete for land and wealth." _____

5. "I was the first explorer of my time to actually set foot in Asia."

   _____

6. "A German mapmaker named a continent after me." _____

7. "I was looking for gold on an isthmus, but I found something else that was just as important." _____

8. "I led the first expedition that sailed around the world."

   _____

9. "When I reached what I thought was China, I saw many white bears and very large stags that looked like horses." _____

10. "I did not find the large cities or the wealthy rulers of Asia that I had read about in books." _____

CALIFORNIA STANDARDS HSS 5.2, 5.2.2

© Harcourt

Use after reading Chapter 3, Lesson 2, pages 120–125.

Name _____ Date _____

Spanish Explorations

DIRECTIONS Use the map to answer the questions that follow about the routes of Spanish explorers and the distances they traveled.

Conquistadors in North America

Legend:
- -◄- - - Ponce de León, 1513
- ◄——— Cortés, 1519
- ◄••••• De Soto, 1539–1542
- ◄-•-•- Coronado, 1540–1542
- ——— Present-day border

1. Which conquistador traveled the longest distance on land? _____

2. Which conquistador crossed the Mississippi River? _____

3. Which conquistadors reached the Arkansas River? _____

4. Which conquistador traveled the farthest north? _____

5. Which conquistadors traveled through present-day Mexico?

_____

6. Which conquistador started his exploration in Puerto Rico?

_____

CALIFORNIA STANDARDS HSS 5.2, 5.2.3; CS 4

Skills: Distinguish Fact from Opinion

DIRECTIONS Read each statement below. In the space provided, write *F* if the statement is a fact. Write *O* if the statement is an opinion.

1 _____ Juan Ponce de León was foolish if he thought that he would find the Fountain of Youth.

2 _____ Juan Ponce de León may have heard that there was a Fountain of Youth on Bimini.

3 _____ Hernando Cortés wanted the Aztecs' gold.

4 _____ I think that Hernando Cortés was a good leader.

5 _____ Hernando Cortés was a terrible man for conquering the Aztecs.

6 _____ Juan Ponce de León was the first Spanish explorer to visit what is now the United States.

DIRECTIONS Write one fact and one opinion about each conquistador named below.

Francisco Vásquez de Coronado

7 Fact: _____

_____

8 Opinion: _____

_____

Hernando de Soto

9 Fact: _____

_____

10 Opinion: _____

_____

© Harcourt

CALIFORNIA STANDARDS HSS 5.2, 5.2.1, 5.2.2

Other Nations Explore

DIRECTIONS Imagine that you are Giovanni da Verrazano and you are being interviewed by a newspaper reporter. Write answers to the interview questions.

1 Mr. Verrazano, what was the aim of your voyages to the west?

_____

_____

_____

2 Who sent you to find the Northwest Passage?

_____

_____

_____

3 What was the biggest obstacle that you faced?

_____

_____

_____

4 You did not achieve your goal, but what did you accomplish?

_____

_____

_____

5 What were these people like?

_____

_____

_____

CALIFORNIA STANDARDS HSS 5.2, 5.2.2

Skills: Use an Elevation Map

DIRECTIONS Add details to the map as described in each item below.

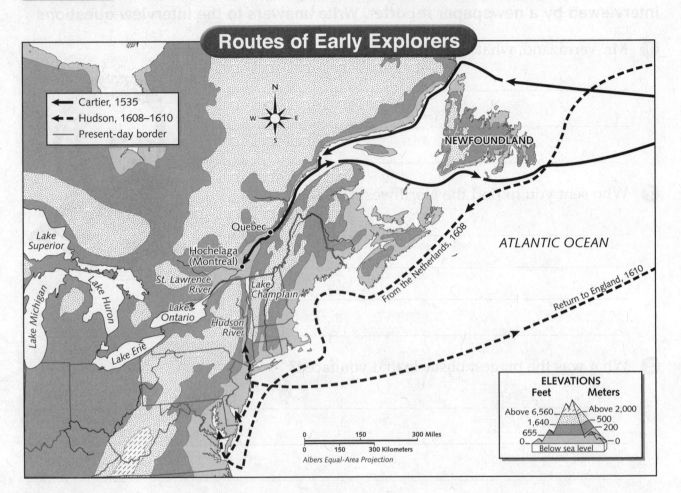

Routes of Early Explorers

Cartier, 1535
Hudson, 1608–1610
Present-day border

Lake Superior
Lake Michigan
Lake Huron
Lake Erie
Lake Ontario
St. Lawrence River
Quebec
Hochelaga (Montreal)
Lake Champlain
Hudson River
NEWFOUNDLAND
ATLANTIC OCEAN
From the Netherlands, 1608
Return to England, 1610

0   150   300 Miles
0   150   300 Kilometers
Albers Equal-Area Projection

ELEVATIONS
Feet   Meters
Above 6,560   Above 2,000
1,640   500
655   200
0   0
Below sea level

1 Write an *H* on any part of the map that shows the highest elevation in the region.

_____

_____

2 Write an *L* on any part of the map that shows the lowest elevation in the region.

_____

_____

CALIFORNIA STANDARDS HSS 5.2; CS 4   *(continued)*

DIRECTIONS **Use the map on page 30 to answer these questions.**

3 What is the range of elevation where the city of Montreal is located?

_____

4 What is the highest range of elevation to the north of Quebec?

_____

5 What was the range of elevation for the water route taken by Cartier from Quebec to Montreal?

_____

_____

6 How would land elevation have changed if Cartier had traveled 150 miles west from Montreal?

_____

_____

7 How would you describe the land elevation to the east of Hudson's route shown on the Hudson River?

_____

_____

8 How would you describe the land elevation to the west of Hudson's route shown on the Hudson River?

_____

_____

9 What kind of landform would you expect to find at the highest elevations to the west of Hudson's route?

_____

_____

10 Write a sentence describing the land that the Hudson River flows through.

_____

_____

Name _____ Date _____

Study Guide

DIRECTIONS Fill in the missing information in these paragraphs about European exploration of the Americas. Use the terms below to help you complete the paragraph for each lesson.

Lesson 1	Lesson 2	Lesson 3	Lesson 4
technology	isthmus	missionaries	St. Lawrence River
benefits	Ferdinand Magellan	grants	mutinied
navigation	Amerigo Vespucci	conquistadors	Northwest Passage
expedition	Newfoundland		
entrepreneur			

Lesson 1   In the 1400s, Europeans entered into a new age of learning, science, and art called the Renaissance. They read about the riches of Asia, but they lacked the knowledge and the tools to reach Asia by sea. To help solve these problems Prince Henry of Portugal started a school to teach _____. People at the school developed new kinds of _____, including better compasses and astrolabes. Christopher Columbus led an _____ with the goal of sailing west to Asia. Like other explorers, Columbus was an _____. He persuaded Queen Isabella to pay for his journey by promising her _____ such as riches from Asia.

CALIFORNIA STANDARDS HSS 5.2, 5.2.1, 5.2.2, 5.2.3

(continued)

© Harcourt

Name _____ Date _____

Lesson 2   Other explorers followed Columbus across the Atlantic.

Giovanni Caboto sailed west to present-day _____.

Caboto thought that he had reached Asia. _____

knew that Caboto was wrong, though. He realized that Caboto and

other explorers had found a continent unknown to Europeans. It

was Vasco Núñez de Balboa who found the key to reaching Asia. He

crossed an _____ and saw the Pacific Ocean.

_____ was the first European to cross the Pacific Ocean

and reach Asia.

Lesson 3   The ruler of Spain wanted explorers to find riches in lands that

Spain had claimed. Spain offered _____ to men who

were willing to lead expeditions to the Americas. These men were known as

_____ . The Catholic Church also wanted to extend its

power to the Americas. For that reason, it sent _____ to

convert American Indians.

Lesson 4   Other explorers still hoped to find a water route to Asia. This route

became known as the _____ . Jacques Cartier traveled

up the _____ , hoping that it would lead to Asia. Henry

Hudson explored other rivers and bays with the same goal. Hudson failed,

and his crew _____ and set him adrift.

READING SOCIAL STUDIES: MAIN IDEA AND DETAILS

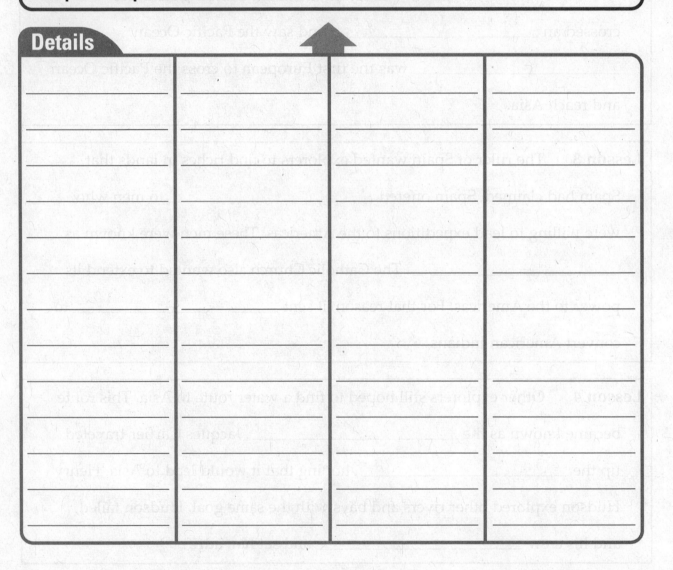

⭐ Focus Skill The Age of Exploration

DIRECTIONS Complete this graphic organizer to show that you understand the main idea and supporting details about European explorations of the Americas.

Main Idea

Europeans explored and claimed lands in the Americas.

Details

CALIFORNIA STANDARDS HSS 5.2, 5.2.1, 5.2.2. 5.2.3

34 ▪ Homework and Practice Book   Use after reading Chapter 3, pages 110–145.

© Harcourt

The Spanish Colonies

DIRECTIONS Read the paragraph. Then answer the questions below.

Santa Fe, New Mexico

In 1598, Juan de Oñate led a large group of people from Mexico north to what would become the Spanish colony of New Mexico. They made the long, difficult journey in search of golden cities. They did not find them, but many people stayed and settled in the area. In 1610, they built a city high on a plateau, where the climate was cooler than it was in the surrounding desert. They named the city Santa Fe, which is Spanish for "holy faith." It was the first permanent European settlement in western North America. In the years after Santa Fe was founded, new settlers and missionaries added to its population. Santa Fe became the capital of Spain's vast territory in New Mexico.

1 Who led the first settlers to New Mexico? _____

2 What city was the capital of New Mexico? _____

3 Why did Europeans first travel to New Mexico? _____

_____

4 Why did the settlers build their city on a plateau? _____

_____

5 When was the first permanent European settlement in western North America

built? _____

CALIFORNIA STANDARDS HSS 5.2.2

The Virginia Colony

DIRECTIONS Complete the organizer to show important facts about the settlers who founded Jamestown.

The Founding of Jamestown

Who	What	When	Where	Why

DIRECTIONS Using the lines provided, write one fact that tells how each person was important to the survival of the Jamestown settlers.

John Smith

_____

_____

Pocahontas

_____

_____

John Rolfe

_____

_____

CALIFORNIA STANDARDS HSS 5.2, 5.2.2, 5.4, 5.4.2; HI 2 *(continued)*

Name _____ Date _____

DIRECTIONS Use your completed organizer to help you write a narrative about life in early Jamestown. Your narrative may include facts that are not on the organizer.

_____

_____

_____

_____

_____

_____

John Smith   **Pocahontas**

_____

_____

_____

_____

_____

_____

_____

_____

_____

_____

_____

_____

_____

_____

_____

Skills: Compare Primary and Secondary Sources

DIRECTIONS Study the photo and illustration below, and use the information they contain to answer questions about primary and secondary sources.

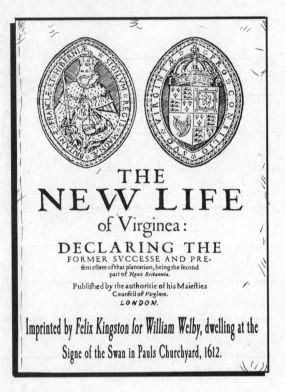

THE
NEW LIFE
of Virginea:
DECLARING THE
FORMER SVCCESSE AND PRE-
fent eftate of that plantation, being the fecond
part of *Nowa Britannia*.
Publifhed by the authoritie of his Maiefties
Counfell of *Virginea*.
LONDON.

Imprinted by *Felix Kingston* for *William Welby*, dwelling at the
Signe of the Swan in Pauls Churchyard, 1612.

1 Is the title page of the book shown a primary or a secondary source? How can you tell?

_____

_____

2 How can you tell that the picture of the Virginia settler is a secondary source?

_____

3 What do the two sources have in common?

_____

CALIFORNIA STANDARDS HSS 5.2.2, 5.3; HR 1   *(continued)*

38 ■ Homework and Practice Book   Use after reading Chapter 4, Skill Lesson, pages 168–169.

Name _____ Date _____

DIRECTIONS This modern drawing shows what the houses built outside the Jamestown fort may have looked like in the early 1600s. Use it to answer the questions that follow.

4 Why did Jamestown settlers have fields so close to their homes?

_____

_____

5 Is the drawing of Jamestown a primary or a secondary source? Explain why.

_____

_____

_____

The Plymouth Colony

DIRECTIONS When the Mayflower Compact was written in 1620, the English language was very different from what it is today. Below is a version of the Mayflower Compact written in present-day language. Use it to answer the questions that follow.

The Mayflower Compact

In the name of God, Amen. We, the loyal subjects of King James and the people of God, have taken a voyage to settle in the first colony in the northern parts of Virginia. We, the people whose names are signed below, have made agreement, in the presence of God and one another, to establish our own government of fair and equal laws. These laws will be decided by the majority rule of this group. These laws are made for the good of the people in the colony as well as for the colony itself. We promise to obey the laws we have made. We have signed our names below, at Cape Cod, on November 11, 1620.

Myles Standish   *William Bradford*

1 Who is the English ruler named in the Mayflower Compact?

_____

2 Where did the Mayflower passengers think they were going to settle?

_____

3 How did the writers of the Mayflower Compact say laws would be decided?

_____

4 What did the passengers promise?

_____

5 Where and when was the Mayflower Compact signed?

_____

CALIFORNIA STANDARDS HSS 5.4, 5.4.5

Use after reading Chapter 4, Lesson 3, pages 170–175.

© Harcourt

The French and the Dutch

DIRECTIONS Read each question below and choose the best answer. Then fill in the circle for the answer you have chosen.

1. Why did French merchants help set up settlements in North America?
   A They wanted the Indians' gold.
   B They wanted wealth from the fur trade.
   C They wanted to control the route to Asia.
   D They wanted to force the Spanish off their land.

2. What kept Marquette and Joliet from reaching the mouth of the Mississippi River?
   A They got lost.
   B They ran out of food.
   C They were attacked by Indians.
   D They feared meeting Spanish soldiers.

3. Who was the first French explorer to reach the mouth of the Mississippi River?
   A Jacques Cartier
   B Samuel de Champlain
   C Sieur de la Salle
   D Pierre Le Moyne

4. What was one problem that early French settlements faced?
   A Few French people wanted to settle in North America.
   B Indians refused to trade with the French.
   C Spanish soldiers attacked French forts.
   D Colonies grew quickly, and good land was scarce.

5. What was the aim of Dutch settlers coming to North America?
   A to make money by selling furs
   B to find good farmland
   C to escape war in Europe
   D to practice their religion

© Harcourt

CALIFORNIA STANDARDS HSS 5.2, 5.2.2

Skills: Read a Historical Map

DIRECTIONS Use the map on this page to help you answer the questions on page 43.

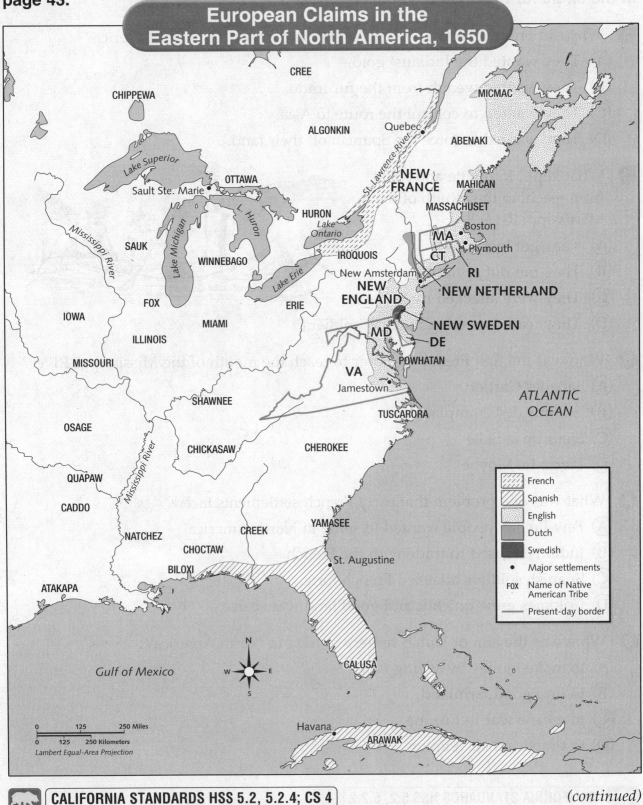

European Claims in the Eastern Part of North America, 1650

Legend:
- French
- Spanish
- English
- Dutch
- Swedish
- • Major settlements
- FOX — Name of Native American Tribe
- Present-day border

CREE
CHIPPEWA
MICMAC
ALGONKIN — Quebec
ABENAKI
Lake Superior
OTTAWA
Sault Ste. Marie
NEW FRANCE
MAHICAN
MASSACHUSET
HURON
Boston
MA
Plymouth
Lake Ontario
CT
IROQUOIS
RI
New Amsterdam
NEW ENGLAND
NEW NETHERLAND
Lake Erie
ERIE
SAUK
WINNEBAGO
Lake Michigan
L. Huron
Mississippi River
FOX
IOWA
MIAMI
NEW SWEDEN
MD
DE
ILLINOIS
POWHATAN
MISSOURI
VA
Jamestown
ATLANTIC OCEAN
SHAWNEE
OSAGE
TUSCARORA
CHICKASAW
CHEROKEE
QUAPAW
Mississippi River
CADDO
YAMASEE
CREEK
NATCHEZ
CHOCTAW
BILOXI
St. Augustine
ATAKAPA
Gulf of Mexico
CALUSA
N W E S
0 125 250 Miles
0 125 250 Kilometers
Lambert Equal-Area Projection
Havana
ARAWAK

CALIFORNIA STANDARDS HSS 5.2, 5.2.4; CS 4

(continued)

© Harcourt

Name _____ Date _____

① What time in history does the map show? _____

② What were the major settlements in Spanish areas? _____
_____

③ What country controlled the St. Lawrence River? _____

④ What country claimed land where the Powhatan lived? _____

⑤ What country claimed land near to where the Huron lived? _____

⑥ Who settled the land known as New Netherland? _____

⑦ What American Indian group lived in the southern part of what is now the state of Florida?
_____

⑧ Which country's settlements extended farthest north?
_____

⑨ Which country claimed the most land? _____

⑩ Describe the location of Swedish settlements relative to the settlements of New England.
_____
_____

Chapter 4

Name _____ Date _____

Study Guide

DIRECTIONS Fill in the missing information in these paragraphs about the first colonies. Use the terms below to help you complete the paragraph for each lesson.

Lesson 1	**Lesson 2**	**Lesson 3**	**Lesson 4**
haciendas	raw materials	Samoset	New Orleans
presidios	cash crop	Tisquantum	Quebec
plantations	royal colony	William Bradford	New Amsterdam
missions	legislature		
borderlands			

Lesson 1   Some early Spanish settlers hoped to find gold, and others

started large farms. However, there was a shortage of workers to do the labor

necessary on a large farm. To find the workers they needed, some Spanish

settlers enslaved Indians to work on these _____. Spanish

soldiers built _____ to protect lands on the edge of New

Spain. Ranchers built large estates, or _____, in the out-

lying lands. Spain did not want to lose these _____ to

other countries. The Spanish also built _____, where

Spanish priests and Indians lived side by side.

CALIFORNIA STANDARDS HSS 5.2, 5.2.2, 5.3, 5.3.1, 5.3.3   *(continued)*

© Harcourt

Name _____ Date _____

Lesson 2 England hoped to profit from _____, such as lumber, from its Virginia Colony. The colonists themselves made money from tobacco, a _____ that they sold to England. As the colony grew, it needed laws. The Virginia _____ was the first representative assembly in the English colonies. After the Powhatan Wars, though, King James I took over Virginia, making it a _____.

Lesson 3 The Pilgrims settled in Massachusetts, where they had religious freedom. They had good leaders, including _____, who invited neighboring Indians to share the first harvest. The Indians were helpful to the Pilgrims. An Abenaki Indian named _____ visited the Pilgrims. He brought a Wampanoag Indian named _____, who taught the settlers how to farm and fish.

Lesson 4 Samuel de Champlain built _____, the first French settlement in North America. French settlements grew slowly. More than 100 years passed before the city of _____ was founded and became the capital of France's southern colony, Louisiana. The Dutch competed with the French for the fur trade. The first Dutch colony was New Netherland, and its main trading center was _____.

© Harcourt

READING SOCIAL STUDIES: MAIN IDEA AND DETAILS

⭐ Focus Skill The First Colonies

DIRECTIONS Complete this graphic organizer to show that you understand the main idea and some supporting details about the first European colonies in the Americas.

Main Idea

Europeans started colonies in North America.

Details

CALIFORNIA STANDARDS HSS 5.2, 5.2.2

46 ▪ Homework and Practice Book   Use after reading Chapter 4, pages 154–185.

© Harcourt

Settling New England

DIRECTIONS Read each statement below. On the blank provided, write the name of the person whom the statement describes. You may use some names more than once.

Thomas Hooker	Anne Hutchinson	Metacomet
David Thomson	Roger Williams	John Winthrop

1 This person lived with the Narragansett Indians after being expelled from the Massachusetts Colony. _____

2 This person founded a fishing village that became part of the New Hampshire Colony. _____

3 This person was a leader of the group that settled Boston.

_____

4 This person became a leader in the Connecticut Colony. _____

5 This person founded a settlement that later joined with Providence and became part of Rhode Island. _____

6 This person helped write the Fundamental Orders. _____

7 This person decided to fight rather than be forced from his land.

_____

8 This person wanted his settlement to be seen by others as an example of Christian living. _____

9 This person was expelled from the Massachusetts Colony after being convicted of sedition. _____

10 This person was elected governor of the Massachusetts Colony.

_____

© Harcourt

CALIFORNIA STANDARDS HSS 5.3, 5.3.3, 5.4, 5.4.2; HI 2

(continued)

Name _____ Date _____

DIRECTIONS Fill in the blanks to complete the web about settling New England.

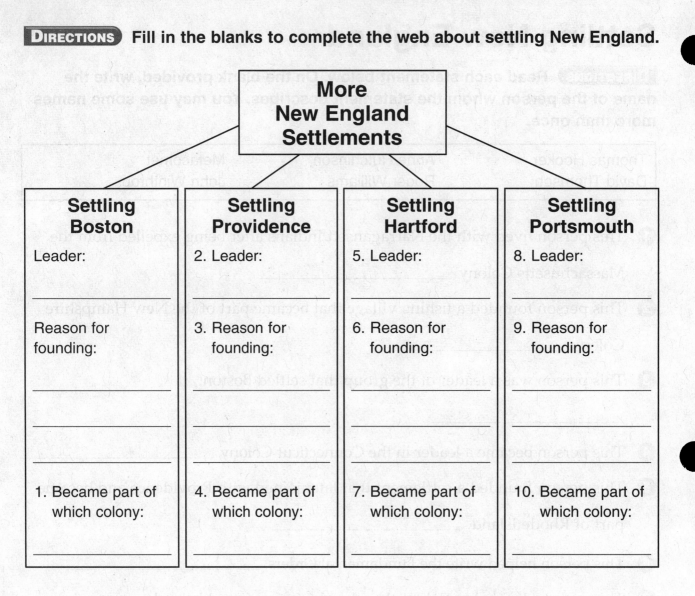

More New England Settlements

Settling Boston

Leader:

_____

Reason for founding:

_____

_____

_____

1. Became part of which colony:

_____

Settling Providence

2. Leader:

_____

3. Reason for founding:

_____

_____

_____

4. Became part of which colony:

_____

Settling Hartford

5. Leader:

_____

6. Reason for founding:

_____

_____

_____

7. Became part of which colony:

_____

Settling Portsmouth

8. Leader:

_____

9. Reason for founding:

_____

_____

_____

10. Became part of which colony:

_____

Use after reading Chapter 5, Lesson 1, pages 206–212.

Life in New England

DIRECTIONS Use the Word Bank below to complete the sentences.

voting

praying

quilt-making

scolding

specializing

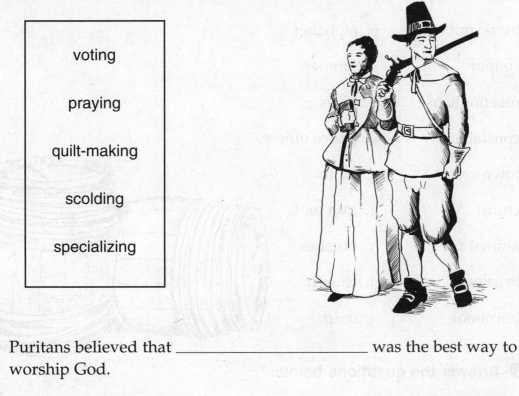

1 Puritans believed that _____ was the best way to worship God.

2 Colonists _____ in various types of work were important to the community.

3 In the New England Colonies, women, indentured servants, and African slaves were not allowed to participate in _____ .

4 _____ was one way that people punished those who missed church.

5 Some children enjoyed sewing and _____ .

© Harcourt

CALIFORNIA STANDARDS HSS 5.4, 5.4.3; CS 3

(continued)

Name _____ Date _____

DIRECTIONS Read each numbered word or phrase. On the line provided, write the letter of the word or phrase that goes with it.

_____ **1** sawmill   a. barrels

_____ **2** blacksmith   b. alphabet

_____ **3** cooper   c. lumber

_____ **4** meetinghouse   d. news

_____ **5** constable   e. police officer

_____ **6** town crier   f. butter

_____ **7** churn   g. iron tools

_____ **8** animal fat   h. brushes

_____ **9** bristles   i. church

_____ **10** hornbook   j. soap

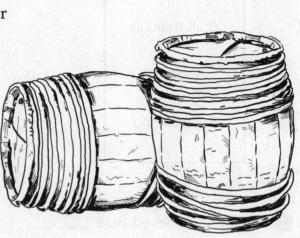

DIRECTIONS Answer the questions below.

1 What did the town crier do?

_____

_____

2 Why was the town crier important?

_____

_____

3 Why is the town crier no longer needed today?

_____

_____

_____

© Harcourt

New England's Economy

DIRECTIONS Use the map to help you answer the questions below.

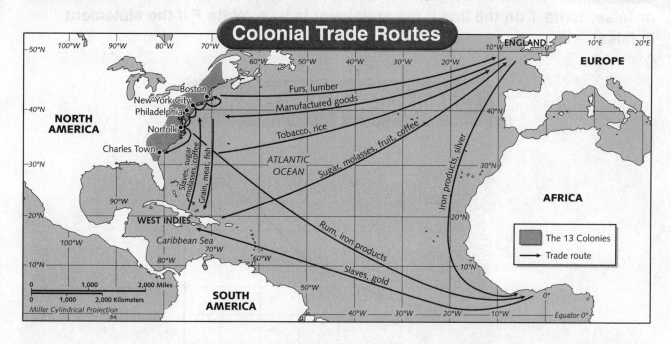

Colonial Trade Routes

① What products did colonists export to Africa? _____

② Besides slaves, what was brought from the West Indies to the colonies?

_____

③ What goods did the New England Colonies export to England?

_____

④ After English ships unloaded iron products and silver in Africa, what was loaded

onto the ships, and where did they go next? _____

_____

⑤ Label the route on the map that includes the Middle Passage.

🐻 **CALIFORNIA STANDARDS HSS 5.4, 5.4.6; CS 4**

Name _____ Date _____

Skills: Read a Line Graph

DIRECTIONS Use the line graph to determine whether each statement is true or false. Write *T* on the line if the statement is true. Write *F* if the statement is false.

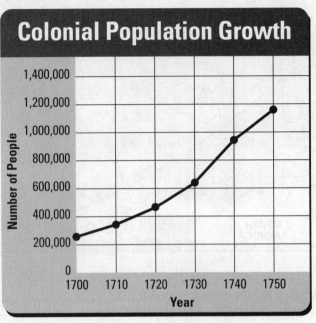

Colonial Population Growth

Source: *Historical Statistics of the United States.*
U.S. Dept. of Commerce, 1975.

_____ **1** There were more than 2 million people in the colonies by 1750.

_____ **2** Between 1700 and 1710, the population grew by fewer than 500,000 people.

_____ **3** There were more than twice as many people in 1740 as there were in 1720.

_____ **4** The population was almost a million people in 1740.

_____ **5** The population decreased between 1710 and 1720.

CALIFORNIA STANDARDS HSS 5.4; CS 1

(continued)

52 ■ **Homework and Practice Book**   Use after reading Chapter 5, Skill Lesson, pages 230–231.

© Harcourt

Name _____   Date _____

DIRECTIONS **Use the line graph on page 52 to help you answer the questions below.**

6 What is the topic, or main idea, of the line graph?

_____

_____

7 What kind of information do the numbers along the left side of the graph give?

_____

8 What period of time separates the dates along the bottom of the graph?

_____

9 In which period of time did population grow the most? How do you know?

_____

_____

10 Write one sentence that summarizes what the graph shows.

_____

_____

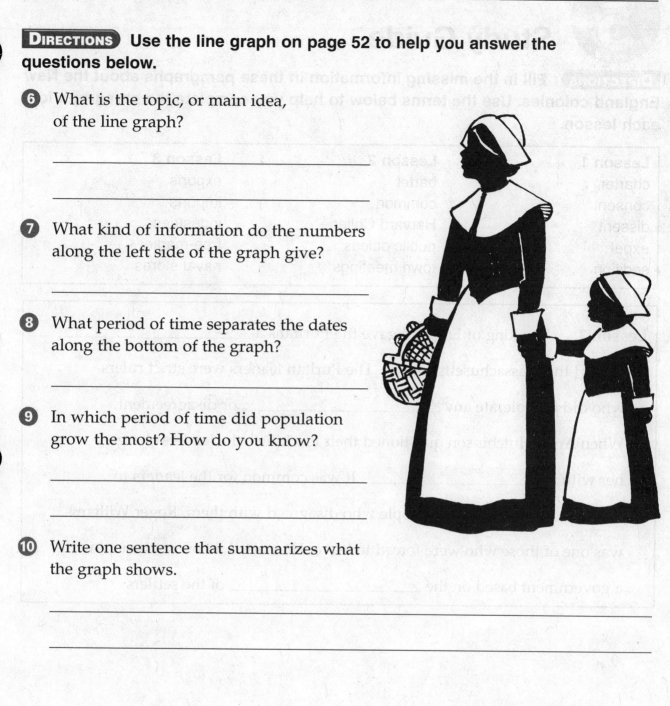

Chapter 5

Name _____ Date _____

Study Guide

DIRECTIONS Fill in the missing information in these paragraphs about the New England colonies. Use the terms below to help you complete the paragraph for each lesson.

Lesson 1	Lesson 2	Lesson 3
charter	barter	exports
consent	common	imports
dissent	Harvard College	industries
expel	public offices	free-market
sedition	town meetings	naval stores

Lesson 1   The king of England gave the Puritans a _____

to start the Massachusetts Colony. The Puritan leaders were strict rulers

who did not tolerate any _____, or disagreement.

When Anne Hutchinson questioned their teachings, the leaders charged

her with _____ . It was common for the leaders to

_____ people who disagreed with them. Roger Williams

was one of those who were forced to leave. He started a new settlement with

a government based on the _____ of the settlers.

CALIFORNIA STANDARDS HSS 5.4, 5.4.2, 5.4.3, 5.4.5   *(continued)*

© Harcourt

Name _____ Date _____

Lesson 2   The Puritans lived and worked together in small towns. At

_____, they took care of all government business.

Every year, they elected people to _____. To meet their

economic needs, the Puritans would _____ with each

other for goods and services. They all shared the _____,

which was used for grazing cattle and sheep. They also shared in

the belief that schools were important. In 1636, the Puritans founded

_____ to train ministers.

Lesson 3   New England colonists developed a _____

economy in which people could compete in business and set their own

prices. The region's _____ included logging and fishing.

Some logs were used to produce the _____ needed to

build and repair ships. Trade was also an important part of the economy.

_____ included grain, furs, whale oil, and other products.

Most _____, or goods brought into the colonies, were

English-made.

Name _____ Date _____

READING SOCIAL STUDIES: SUMMARIZE

Focus Skill ⭐ Religion in New England

DIRECTIONS Complete this graphic organizer to show that you can summarize the role of religion in the New England Colonies.

Key Fact

_____
_____
_____
_____

Key Fact

_____
_____
_____

Key Fact

_____
_____
_____

Summary

Religion shaped life in the New England Colonies.

CALIFORNIA STANDARDS HSS 5.4, 5.4.3

© Harcourt

Use after reading Chapter 5, pages 206–231.

Settling the Middle Colonies

DIRECTIONS Read each description. Write its number on the map in the colony it describes. Also, fill in the blanks below each description with the name of the correct colony.

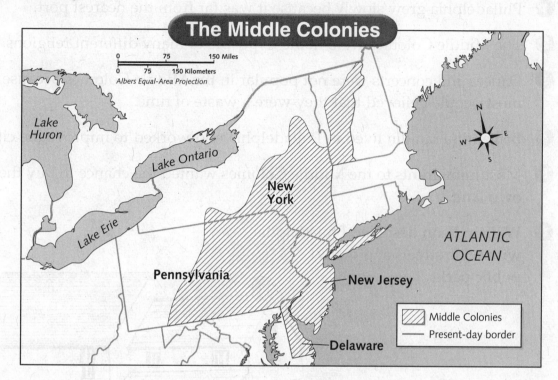

The Middle Colonies

1. The first Quaker settlement in North America was founded here.

_____

2. Settlers of this colony asked William Penn for their own assembly.

_____

3. James, Duke of York, gave this land to John Berkeley and George Carteret.

_____

4. William Penn's frame of government gave its citizens important rights.

_____

5. Before its name was changed, it was the Dutch colony of New Netherland.

_____

CALIFORNIA STANDARDS HSS 5.4, 5.4.1

© Harcourt

Life in the Middle Colonies

DIRECTIONS Read each sentence. If the sentence is true, write *T* on the line provided. If the sentence is false, write *F*.

_____ **1** Philadelphia grew slowly because it was far from the nearest port.

_____ **2** The Middle Colonies were home to people of many different religions.

_____ **3** Dances and concerts were not popular in the Middle Colonies because most people believed that they were a waste of time.

_____ **4** Benjamin Franklin lived in Philadelphia and worked to improve the city.

_____ **5** Most immigrants to the Middle Colonies wanted the chance to buy their own land.

_____ **6** William Penn designed Philadelphia with wide streets and many public parks.

CALIFORNIA STANDARDS HSS 5.4, 5.4.1, 5.4.4   *(continued)*

© Harcourt

Name _____ Date _____

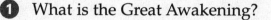

DIRECTIONS Imagine that you are George Whitefield and that you are being interviewed by a newspaper reporter. Answer the questions.

1 What is the Great Awakening?

_____

_____

2 How do your sermons differ from those of more traditional ministers?

_____

_____

3 You are recognized as one of the leaders of the movement. Who else is considered a leader in spreading these ideas?

_____

_____

4 Why has your movement affected so many people?

_____

_____

5 Even though your movement is not popular with all people, how has it affected

religion in the colonies? _____

_____

_____

_____

Busy Farms and Seaports

DIRECTIONS Read each question, and choose the best answer. Then fill in the circle for the answer that you have chosen.

1 What was the name for a young person who was learning a skill?

Ⓐ an apprentice

Ⓑ an artisan

Ⓒ a mason

Ⓓ a tanner

2 Which of the following did the Middle Colonies import from England?

Ⓐ grain

Ⓑ gunpowder

Ⓒ lumber

Ⓓ slaves

3 What happened at a gristmill?

Ⓐ Logs were made into lumber.

Ⓑ Iron was made into horseshoes.

Ⓒ Thread was made into cloth.

Ⓓ Grain was made into flour.

4 Which of the following was NOT important to the prosperity of the Middle Colonies?

Ⓐ farms

Ⓑ trade

Ⓒ whales

Ⓓ ports

5 Which of these workers made finished goods from farm products?

Ⓐ blacksmiths

Ⓑ coopers

Ⓒ masons

Ⓓ bakers

CALIFORNIA STANDARDS HSS 5.4

(continued)

© Harcourt

Name _____ Date _____

deep harbor	Delaware River	fur traders
market towns	skilled trades	artisan households

1 _____ who lived inland floated their goods down rivers to port cities.

2 New York City had a _____ along the East River that offered a good place for ships to dock.

3 Farmers in the Middle Colonies usually traveled to _____ to sell or trade their livestock and crops.

4 Philadelphia grew because of its location on the _____.

5 Some colonists made their living in _____, such as carpentry and shipbuilding.

6 Women and girls had fewer opportunities to work outside the home. However, they often made woven goods or candles that

were sold by _____.

© Harcourt

Skills: Make an Economic Choice

DIRECTIONS Making wise economic choices was an important skill for people living in the Middle Colonies. Most people could not buy everything they wanted at one time. They had to make trade-offs and understand the opportunity costs of their choices. Imagine that you are a farmer in the Middle Colonies. Complete the diagram.

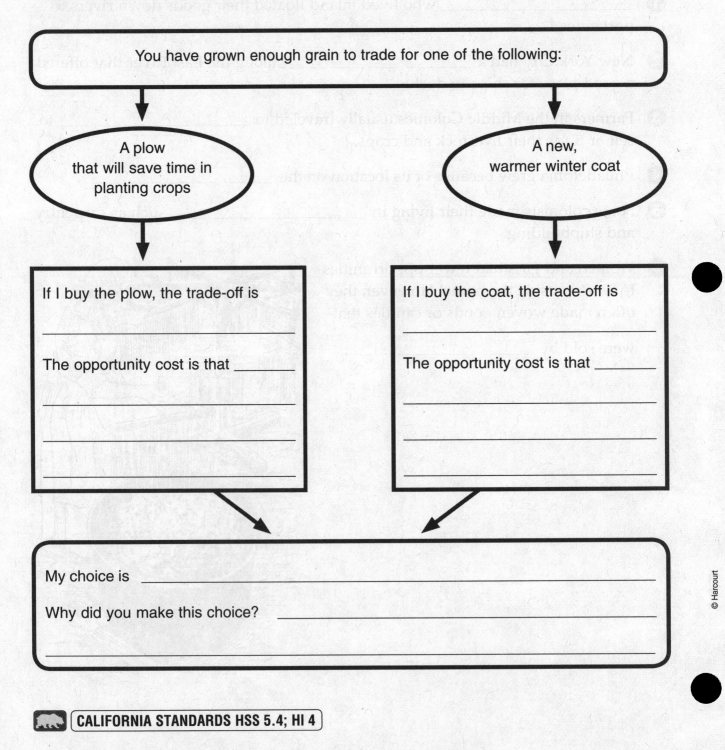

You have grown enough grain to trade for one of the following:

A plow that will save time in planting crops

A new, warmer winter coat

If I buy the plow, the trade-off is
_____

The opportunity cost is that _____
_____
_____
_____

If I buy the coat, the trade-off is
_____

The opportunity cost is that _____
_____
_____
_____

My choice is _____

Why did you make this choice? _____
_____

CALIFORNIA STANDARDS HSS 5.4; HI 4

Chapter 6

Name _____ Date _____

Study Guide

DIRECTIONS   Fill in the missing information in these paragraphs about the Middle Colonies. Use the terms below to help you complete the paragraph for each lesson.

Lesson 1	Lesson 2	Lesson 3
Tamanend	militia	apprentices
refuge	Great Awakening	tanners
James, Duke of York	immigrants	masons
proprietor	Benjamin Franklin	artisans
Peter Stuyvesant	George Whitefield	prosperity

Lesson 1   The Middle Colonies had a diverse population. The Dutch colony

of New Netherland was led by _____. It welcomed

settlers from many countries. In 1664, _____, sent

English warships to seize New Netherland. It became two English colonies,

New York and New Jersey. Quakers found a _____

in New Jersey. William Penn was the _____ of

Pennsylvania. He met with _____ and established

peace with neighboring Indians.

 CALIFORNIA STANDARDS HSS 5.4, 5.4.2, 5.4.3, 5.4.4   *(continued)*

Lesson 2   Philadelphia was the cultural center of the Middle Colonies.

Many _____ arrived there to start new lives. The city

was home to many famous people. _____ helped

start a fire department, a hospital, a library, and a college. He also orga-

nized a _____ to protect the colony. In the 1720s,

the _____ brought a return to religious ways of life.

_____ and other ministers spread their ideas through-

out the Middle Colonies.

Lesson 3   The economy of the Middle Colonies was as diverse as the

region's people. Farming and trade were the main reasons for the region's

_____. But this economic success also created many

other kinds of jobs. _____ used raw materials to make

products from iron tools to barrels. _____ used stone

to construct roads, walls, and buildings. _____ turned

animal skins into leather for shoes and other products. Young people learned

these skills by becoming _____ .

Name _____   Date _____

READING SOCIAL STUDIES: SUMMARIZE
(Focus Skill) The Middle Colonies

DIRECTIONS Complete this graphic organizer to show that you can summarize facts about the Middle Colonies.

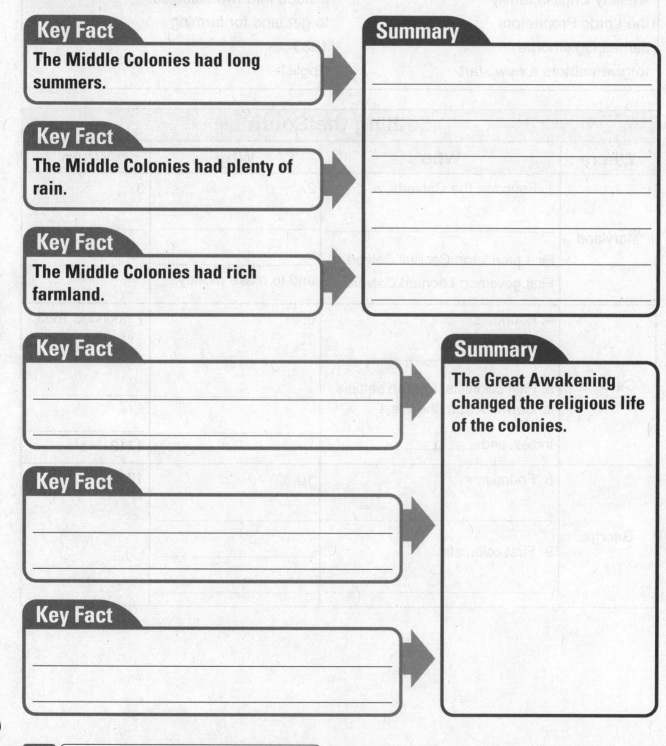

Key Fact

The Middle Colonies had long summers.

Key Fact

The Middle Colonies had plenty of rain.

Key Fact

The Middle Colonies had rich farmland.

Summary

_____
_____
_____
_____
_____
_____

Key Fact

_____
_____

Key Fact

_____
_____

Key Fact

_____
_____

Summary

The Great Awakening changed the religious life of the colonies.

CALIFORNIA STANDARDS HSS 5.4, 5.4.1

© Harcourt

Name _____ Date _____

Settling the South

DIRECTIONS Choose words and phrases from the box to complete the chart.

as a refuge for Catholics	African slaves
wealthy English family	divided into two colonies
the Lords Proprietors	to get land for farming
James Oglethorpe	1633
to give debtors a new start	English

Settling the South			
Where	**Who**	**Why**	**When**
Maryland	1. Founder: the Calverts, a _____ First proprietor: Cecilius Calvert First governor: Leonard Calvert	2. _____ _____ _____ and to make money	3. _____ _____
Carolina	4. Founders: _____ 5. First colonists: English settlers, landowners from the West Indies, and _____	6. _____ _____ _____	7. founded 1663; _____ _____ 1712
Georgia	8. Founder: _____ 9. First colonists: _____	10. _____ _____	1733

CALIFORNIA STANDARDS HSS 5.4, 5.4.1, 5.4.2, 5.4.3; HI 2 *(continued)*

Use after reading Chapter 7, Lesson 1, pages 272–279.

© Harcourt

Name _____   Date _____

DIRECTIONS **Use the completed chart on page 66 to help you answer these questions.**

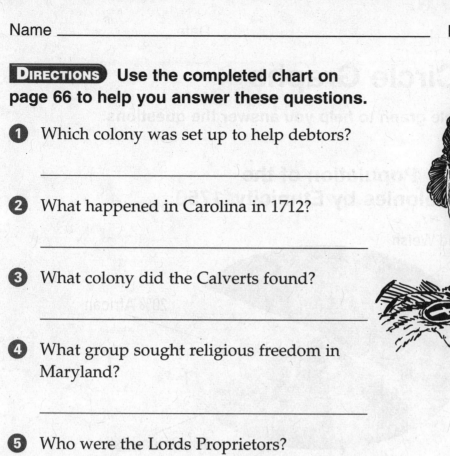

James Oglethorpe

1 Which colony was set up to help debtors?

_____

2 What happened in Carolina in 1712?

_____

3 What colony did the Calverts found?

_____

4 What group sought religious freedom in Maryland?

_____

5 Who were the Lords Proprietors?

_____

6 Which colony was founded 100 years after the Maryland Colony?

_____

7 Who were the Calverts?

_____

8 Where did many colonists settle in order to get land for farming?

_____

9 Who founded the Georgia Colony? When was it founded?

_____

_____

10 In which colony were Africans among the first colonists?

_____

_____

Skills: Read Circle Graphs

DIRECTIONS Use the circle graph to help you answer the questions.

Population of the 13 Colonies by Ethnicity, 1750

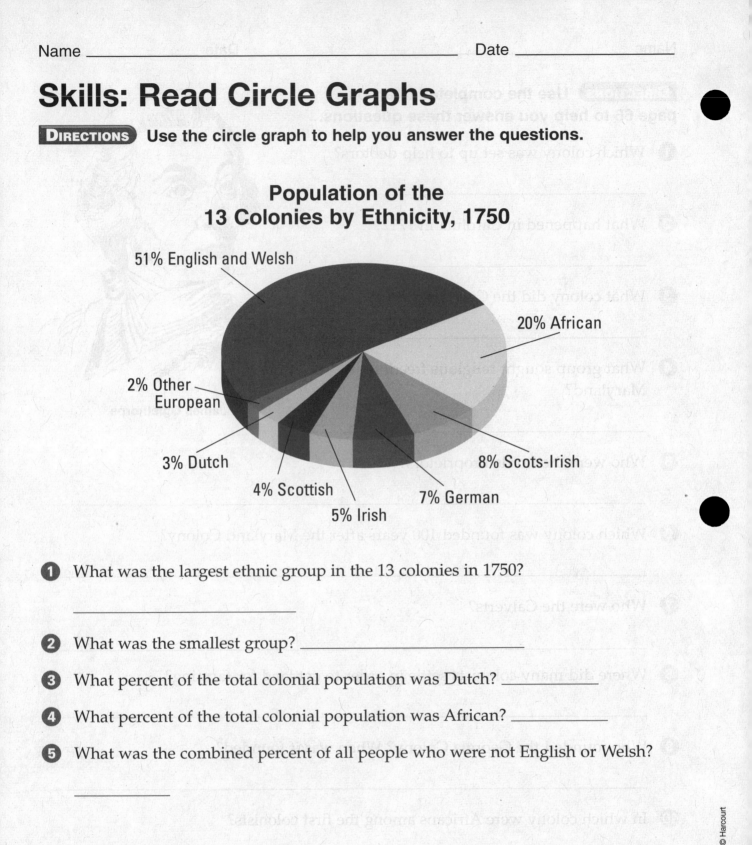

51% English and Welsh

20% African

2% Other European

3% Dutch

4% Scottish

5% Irish

7% German

8% Scots-Irish

1 What was the largest ethnic group in the 13 colonies in 1750?

_____

2 What was the smallest group? _____

3 What percent of the total colonial population was Dutch? _____

4 What percent of the total colonial population was African? _____

5 What was the combined percent of all people who were not English or Welsh?

_____

CALIFORNIA STANDARDS HSS 5.4, 5.4.2, 5.4.3; HI 2   *(continued)*

68 ■ **Homework and Practice Book**   Use after reading Chapter 7, Skill Lesson, pages 280–281.

© Harcourt

Name _____ Date _____

DIRECTIONS Use the information in the table to label the circle graph showing the kinds of churches that Pennsylvania colonists belonged to. Complete the circle graph by labeling each of its parts with the correct letter for the church and the percentage of the population it represented.

| Pennsylvania Churches in 1750* ||
Church	Percent of Population
A. Dutch Reformed	32%
B. Lutheran	28%
C. Baptist	15%
D. Anglican	10%
E. German Reformed	6%
F. Catholic	6%
G. Congregationalist	3%

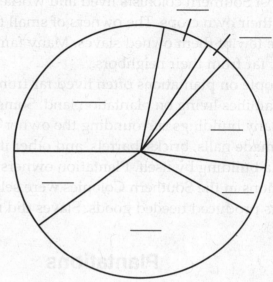

*Quaker meetinghouses not included

DIRECTIONS Use the information in the circle graph to answer these questions.

1 What kind of church had the largest number of members? _____

2 What percent of Pennsylvania colonists were Catholic? _____

3 What other church had about the same number of members as the Catholic

Church? _____

4 What two church groups made up twenty-five percent of Pennsylvania's

population? _____

Life in the South

DIRECTIONS Read the passage below. Use the information it contains to complete the Venn diagram, comparing and contrasting life in the South.

Plantations and Small Farms

Most Southern colonists lived and worked on small farms. They planted and harvested their own crops. The owners of small farms did most of the work themselves, because few of them owned slaves. Many families on small farms lived in one-story houses, far from their neighbors.

People on plantations often lived far from others, too. However, there were often many families living on plantation land. Sometimes plantations looked like small villages, with many buildings surrounding the owner's home. Some were workshops, where slaves made nails, bricks, barrels, and other items used on the plantation. The kitchen was in a building by itself. Plantation owners often lived in large houses. Many of the plantations in the Southern Colonies were self-sufficient. Planters grew food, and skilled workers produced needed goods. Slaves did most of the work on the plantations.

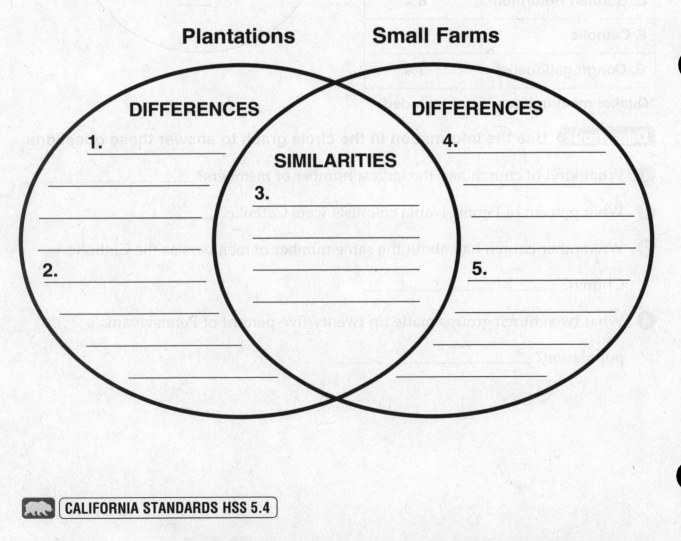

Plantations   **Small Farms**

DIFFERENCES   DIFFERENCES

1. _____   4. _____

_____   _____

SIMILARITIES

3. _____

2. _____   5. _____

_____

_____   _____

_____   _____

CALIFORNIA STANDARDS HSS 5.4

© Harcourt

Name _____ Date _____

The Southern Economy

1 What role did brokers play in the Southern economy? _____

_____

_____

2 What cash crop grew well on warm, wet land? _____

3 Why did the introduction of indigo as a cash crop help the Southern economy?

_____

4 Besides agriculture and trade, what were two industries in the Southern

Colonies? _____

_____

5 How did slaves contribute to the economic success of the Southern Colonies?

_____

_____

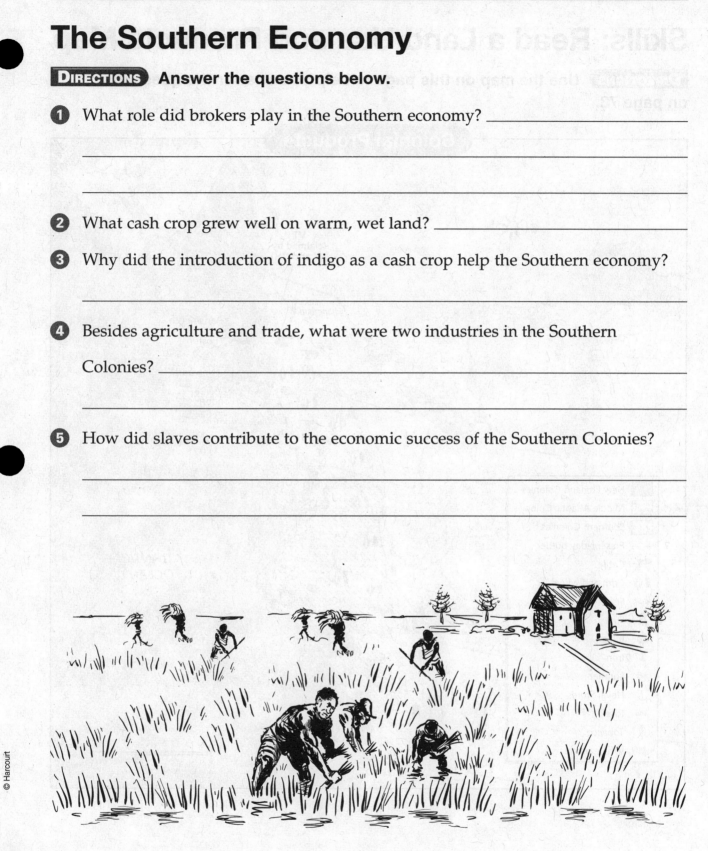

© Harcourt

🐻 **CALIFORNIA STANDARDS HSS 5.4, 5.4.1, 5.4.5, 5.4.6; HI 2**

Skills: Read a Land Use and Products Map

DIRECTIONS Use the map on this page to help you answer the questions on page 73.

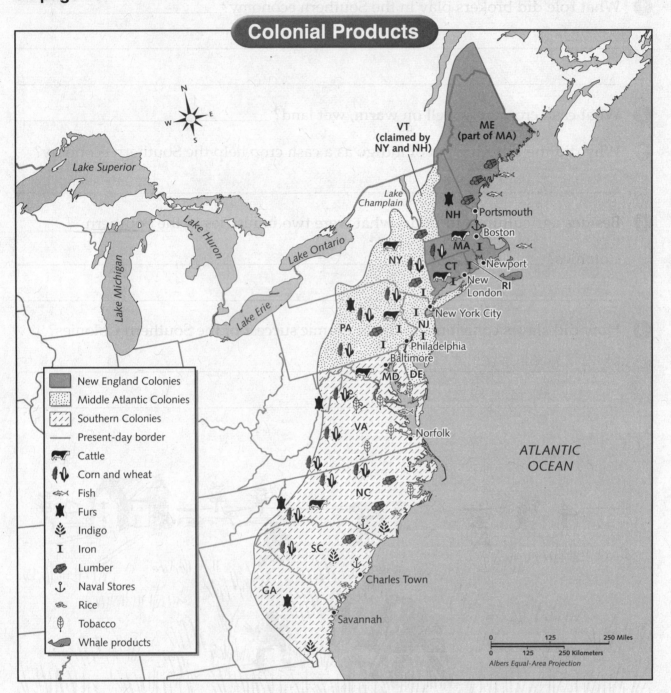

Colonial Products

Legend:
- New England Colonies
- Middle Atlantic Colonies
- Southern Colonies
- Present-day border
- Cattle
- Corn and wheat
- Fish
- Furs
- Indigo
- Iron
- Lumber
- Naval Stores
- Rice
- Tobacco
- Whale products

0   125   250 Miles
0   125   250 Kilometers
Albers Equal-Area Projection

© Harcourt

🐻 **CALIFORNIA STANDARDS HSS 5.4; CS 4**   *(continued)*

Name _____ Date _____

1 Which colonies produced indigo?

_____

2 Where was rice grown? _____

3 Which colonies manufactured iron? _____

_____

4 Which colonies raised cattle? _____

_____

5 In which colonies were you likely to find whale products?

_____

6 Which colonies grew the cash crop tobacco?

_____

7 Which colonies produced naval stores? _____

_____

8 What part of the Massachusetts Colony produced a great deal of lumber and fish?

_____

9 What crops were grown along almost the entire length of the colonies?

_____

10 Which colonies had a great variety of products?

_____

_____

Chapter 7

Name _____ Date _____

Study Guide

DIRECTIONS Fill in the missing information in these paragraphs about the Southern Colonies. Use the terms below to help you complete the paragraph for each lesson.

Lesson 1	Lesson 2	Lesson 3
Maryland	Black Seminoles	shipbuilding
James Oglethorpe	overseers	Charles Town
backcountry	Fort Mose	indigo
constitution	planters	tobacco
Toleration Act	institutionalized	Wilmington

Lesson 1 The Calvert family founded the _____

Colony along Chesapeake Bay. The colony's assembly passed the

_____, which granted religious freedom to

all Christians. The Lords Proprietors founded Carolina and wrote

a _____, or plan of government, for it.

_____ founded Georgia to provide a new home

for English debtors. In the mid-1700s, settlers began to move inland to a

region they called the _____.

CALIFORNIA STANDARDS HSS 5.4, 5.4.1, 5.4.2, 5.4.5, 5.4.6   (continued)

74 ▪ **Homework and Practice Book**   Use after reading Chapter 7, pages 272–297.

© Harcourt

Name _____ Date _____

Lesson 2   Most Southern colonists lived either on plantations or on small

farms. _____ were the wealthiest people in

society. They hired _____ to watch slaves at work

in their fields. In time, slavery became _____ ,

or a part of life, in the colonies. Some slaves escaped from plantations or

bought their freedom. Those who went to live among the Indians were

called _____ . Others started the settlement of

_____ in Spanish Florida.

Lesson 3   Cash crops were important to the Southern economy.

_____ grew in Maryland, Virginia, and northern

North Carolina. Rice and _____ grew farther

south. _____ became an important port city

for shipping rice. Grain and tobacco were shipped from Baltimore, and

_____ was also an important industry in that

city. _____ was an important shipping center for

forest products.

© Harcourt

Name _____ Date _____

READING SOCIAL STUDIES: SUMMARIZE

⭐ **Focus Skill** **Life in the Southern Colonies**

DIRECTIONS Complete this graphic organizer to show that you can summarize facts about the Southern Colonies.

Key Fact
Planters grew cash crops such as tobacco.

Key Fact
Planters traded cash crops for goods and services.

Key Fact
Planters sold their cash crops in England.

Summary

_____
_____
_____
_____
_____
_____
_____

Key Fact

_____
_____

Key Fact

_____
_____

Key Fact

_____
_____

Summary
Enslaved Africans dealt with the hardships of their lives in many ways.

🐻 **CALIFORNIA STANDARDS HSS 5.4**

Use after reading Chapter 7, pages 272–297.

Competition for Control

DIRECTIONS Number the sentences in the order in which the events occurred.

Chief Pontiac

1 _____ To make up for Spain's losses in the war, France gave Spain most of its lands west of the Mississippi River.

2 _____ The British captured several forts, including Fort Duquesne.

3 _____ The French and Indian War ended with the Treaty of Paris, giving Britain most of present-day Canada and all French lands east of the Mississippi River and Spanish Florida.

4 _____ King George III issued the Proclamation of 1763, which said that all land west of the Appalachian Mountains belonged to the Indians.

5 _____ The French built Fort Duquesne at the present-day site of Pittsburgh, Pennsylvania.

6 _____ The French and Indian War began with the battle of Fort Necessity.

7 _____ The French sent soldiers to drive British traders out of the Ohio Valley.

8 _____ The British Parliament passed the Sugar Act, which was designed to make colonists help pay for Britain's defense of the colonies.

9 _____ Chief Pontiac joined with other American Indian tribes and attacked British forts.

10 _____ Colonial leaders rejected Benjamin Franklin's Albany Plan of Union.

CALIFORNIA STANDARDS HSS 5.3, 5.3.1, 5.3.3; CS 1

Skills: Compare Historical Maps

DIRECTIONS Use the maps below to help you answer the questions that follow.

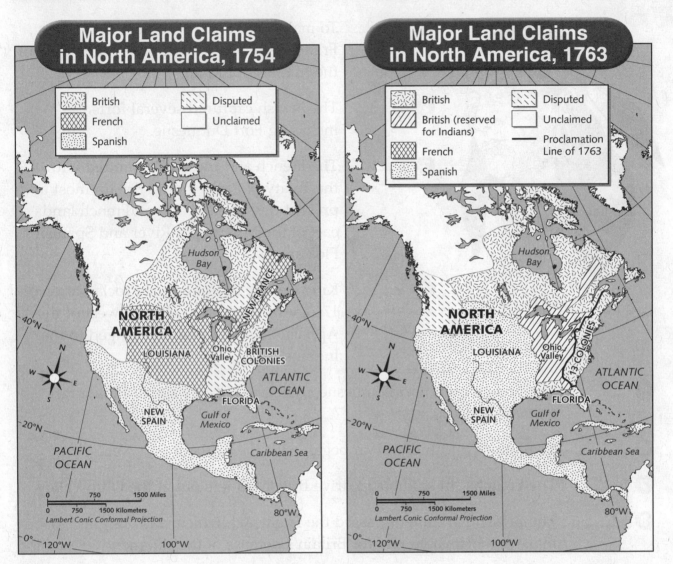

Major Land Claims in North America, 1754

British
French
Spanish
Disputed
Unclaimed

NORTH AMERICA

Hudson Bay

NEW FRANCE

LOUISIANA

Ohio Valley

BRITISH COLONIES

ATLANTIC OCEAN

NEW SPAIN

Gulf of Mexico

FLORIDA

Caribbean Sea

PACIFIC OCEAN

40°N

20°N

0°

120°W

100°W

80°W

0   750   1500 Miles
0   750   1500 Kilometers
Lambert Conic Conformal Projection

Major Land Claims in North America, 1763

British
British (reserved for Indians)
French
Spanish
Disputed
Unclaimed
Proclamation Line of 1763

NORTH AMERICA

Hudson Bay

LOUISIANA

Ohio Valley

13 COLONIES

ATLANTIC OCEAN

NEW SPAIN

Gulf of Mexico

FLORIDA

Caribbean Sea

PACIFIC OCEAN

40°N

20°N

0°

120°W

100°W

80°W

0   750   1500 Miles
0   750   1500 Kilometers
Lambert Conic Conformal Projection

1 Which country claimed Louisiana in 1754?

_____

2 Which countries gained land between 1754 and 1763?

_____

CALIFORNIA STANDARDS HSS 5.3, 5.3.1, 5.3.3; CS 4; HI 3   *(continued)*

78 ■ **Homework and Practice Book**   Use after reading Chapter 8, Skill Lesson, pages 324–325.

3 Which country lost all its lands in North America between 1754 and 1763?

_____

4 What event explains the differences between Map A and Map B?

_____

5 What regions did Britain claim both in 1754 and in 1763?

_____

_____

6 What happened to Louisiana between 1754 and 1763?

_____

7 What two countries claimed land that bordered the disputed area of the Pacific Northwest in 1763?

_____

8 For what group was the land in the Ohio Valley area reserved by King George III?

_____

9 What area changed from Spanish control to British control?

_____

10 Did any areas change from British control to Spanish control?

_____

_____

Name _____ Date _____

Colonists Speak Out

DIRECTIONS Read each numbered description. On the line provided, write the letter of the person, group, or law that goes with it.

1 _____ a tax on colonial newspapers   a. Patrick Henry

2 _____ killed at Boston Massacre   b. James Otis

3 _____ captured British tax collectors   c. Daughters of Liberty

4 _____ a tax on imports to the colonies   d. Crispus Attucks

5 _____ was accused of treason   e. Stamp Act

6 _____ pushed Parliament to tax colonies   f. Benjamin Franklin

7 _____ "No taxation without representation."   g. Sons of Liberty

8 _____ protested tax laws in Parliament   h. George Grenville

9 _____ told colonists not to drink tea   i. Paul Revere

10 _____ made a picture of the Boston Massacre   j. Townshend Acts

Benjamin Franklin

CALIFORNIA STANDARDS HSS 5.5, 5.5.1, 5.5.4

Skills: Distinguish Fact from Fiction

DIRECTIONS Read the passages below about General Washington's crossing of the Delaware River. Then answer the questions.

Passage A   "As the four boys sat huddled together, the oarsmen dressed in tattered blue and buff uniforms used their long poles to push off the ice. Matt recognized them from the history report he and Q had worked on together.

"'They must be John Glover's Marbleheaders!' he whispered to Q.

"'This must be the Delaware River,' Q whispered back. Both boys remembered reading about the special group of seafaring enlisted men from the north, under the guidance of Colonel John Glover of Marblehead, Massachusetts. They had manned the sturdy Durham boats that had carried Washington and his troops across the river on that Christmas night."*

---

*Elvira Woodruff. *George Washington's Socks.* Scholastic, 1991.

Passage B   "I am sitting in the ferry house. The troops are all over, and boats have gone back for the artillery. We are three hours behind the set time . . . [the Marblehead fishermen] directing the boats have had a hard time to force boats through the floating ice with the snow drifting in their faces . . ."*

---

*excerpt from *The Diary of Colonel John Fitzgerald* in *The American Revolution in the Delaware Valley* by Edward S. Gifford, Jr. Pennsylvania Society of Sons of the Revolution, 1976.

1 Which passage is from a documentary source?

_____

2 Which passage is from a fictional source?

_____

3 What is one clue that helped you make your decision?

_____

_____

_____

CALIFORNIA STANDARDS HSS 5.5, 5.5.4; HR 3

Disagreements Grow

DIRECTIONS Answer the following questions about the First Continental Congress.

1 How did the First Continental Congress get its name?

_____

_____

2 Why did the First Continental Congress meet?

_____

_____

3 Where did the First Continental Congress meet?

_____

_____

4 In its signed petition to the king, what rights did the First Continental Congress claim colonists had?

_____

_____

_____

5 The First Continental Congress asked the British Parliament to respond to its petition by what date?

_____

_____

6 How did the First Continental Congress make war with Britain more likely?

_____

_____

_____

© Harcourt

CALIFORNIA STANDARDS HSS 5.5, 5.5.2; HI 1

Name _____ Date _____

The Road to War

DIRECTIONS Choose the phrase from the box that best completes each sentence. Write the phrase in the blank.

Olive Branch Petition	Continental currency
Continental Army	Bunker Hill
Second Continental Congress	

1 The _____ met as a result of the fighting at Lexington and Concord.

2 The _____ differed from militias in that it was made up of full-time soldiers.

3 The _____ asked Britain's King George III for peace on behalf of the colonists.

4 As part of its preparations for war, Congress printed

_____.

5 After the battle at _____, the king sent a proclamation promising to crush the rebellion in the colonies.

Declaring Independence

DIRECTIONS Read each sentence below. On the line provided, write the name of the person whom the sentence tells about.

John Adams	John Dickinson	John Hancock
Thomas Paine	Thomas Jefferson	Richard Henry Lee

1 "I told the Second Continental Congress that the 13 colonies no longer owed any loyalty to the British king."

_____

2 "I was the president of the Second Continental Congress and the first person to sign the Declaration of Independence."

_____

3 "I was the main writer of the Declaration of Independence."

_____

4 "I thought that Americans should always celebrate Independence Day."

_____

5 "I wrote *Common Sense*, which said that people should rule themselves."

_____

6 "I headed the committee that wrote the Articles of Confederation."

_____

CALIFORNIA STANDARDS HSS 5.5, 5.5.3, 5.5.4

Use after reading Chapter 8, Lesson 5, pages 348–353.

Name _____ Date _____

Skills: Identify Multiple Causes and Their Effects

DIRECTIONS Using the chart below, answer questions about causes and effects.

The Declaration of Independence

Causes

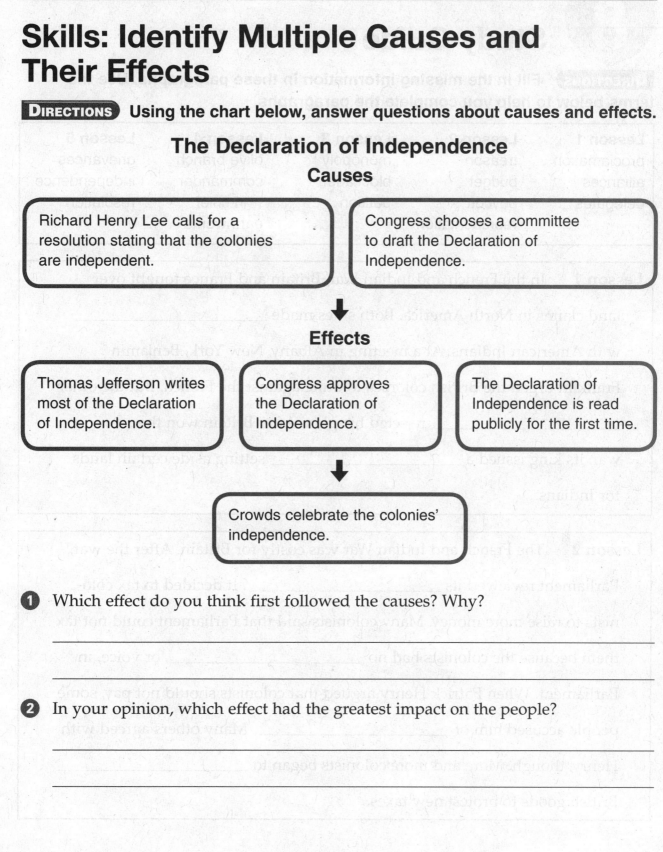

Richard Henry Lee calls for a resolution stating that the colonies are independent.

Congress chooses a committee to draft the Declaration of Independence.

Effects

Thomas Jefferson writes most of the Declaration of Independence.

Congress approves the Declaration of Independence.

The Declaration of Independence is read publicly for the first time.

Crowds celebrate the colonies' independence.

1 Which effect do you think first followed the causes? Why?

_____

_____

2 In your opinion, which effect had the greatest impact on the people?

_____

_____

CALIFORNIA STANDARDS HSS 5.5, 5.5.1; HI 3

Name _____ Date _____

Study Guide

DIRECTIONS   Fill in the missing information in these paragraphs. Use the terms below to help you complete the paragraphs.

Lesson 1	Lesson 2	Lesson 3	Lesson 4	Lesson 5
proclamation	treason	monopoly	olive branch	grievances
alliances	budget	blockade	commander	independence
delegates	boycott	petition	in chief	resolution
	representation		earthworks	

Lesson 1   In the French and Indian War, Britain and France fought over

land claims in North America. Both sides made _____

with American Indians. At a meeting in Albany, New York, Benjamin

Franklin urged the British colonies to unite against the French. But the other

_____ rejected his plan. After Britain won the

war, its king issued a _____ setting aside certain lands

for Indians.

Lesson 2   The French and Indian War was costly for Britain. After the war,

Parliament reviewed its _____ . It decided to tax colo-

nists to raise more money. Many colonists said that Parliament could not tax

them because the colonists had no _____ , or voice, in

Parliament. When Patrick Henry argued that colonists should not pay, some

people accused him of _____ . Many others agreed with

Henry, though. More and more colonists began to _____

British goods to protest new taxes.

CALIFORNIA STANDARDS HSS 5.3, 5.3.3, 5.5, 5.5.1, 5.5.2, 5.5.3, 5.5.4   *(continued)*

Use after reading Chapter 8, pages 318–357.

Lesson 3   The Tea Act gave Britain a _____ on tea in the colonies. In response, the Sons of Liberty threw boxes of British tea into Boston Harbor. British leaders were so angry that they ordered the navy to _____ the harbor. Colonial leaders met at the First Continental Congress and decided to send a _____ to the king, stating colonists' rights.

Lesson 4   The Second Continental Congress set up the Continental Army and named George Washington its _____. The war's first major battle, at Lexington and Concord, had already taken place. At Breed's Hill, colonists fired at British soldiers from defenses called _____. The British won Breed's Hill, but more than 1,000 British soldiers died. Afterwards, Congress asked King George III for peace. Its petition was named after the _____, an ancient symbol of peace.

Lesson 5   As conflicts between Britain and the colonies grew, more and more colonists wanted _____ from Britain. In Congress, Richard Henry Lee called for a _____ to free the united colonies. Congress chose a committee to write to King George III about the matter. This statement became known as the Declaration of Independence. It listed many _____, or complaints, that the colonists had against the king and Parliament.

© Harcourt

READING SOCIAL STUDIES: CAUSE AND EFFECT

⭐ **Focus Skill** **Uniting the Colonies**

DIRECTIONS Complete this graphic organizer to show that you understand some of the causes and effects of the American Revolution.

Cause

Britain needed money to pay for the French and Indian War.

➤ **Effect**

_____

_____

Cause

_____

_____

➤ **Effect**

Colonists staged the Boston Tea Party.

Cause

Britain passed the Intolerable Acts.

➤ **Effect**

_____

_____

Cause

British soldiers and colonists often clashed in Boston.

➤ **Effect**

_____

_____

© Harcourt

CALIFORNIA STANDARDS HSS 5.5, 5.5.1

Use after reading Chapter 8, pages 318–357.

Americans and the Revolution

DIRECTIONS   Read each statement below. On the line provided, write *P* if the statement is something that a Patriot would have said. Write *L* if the statement is something that a Loyalist would have said, and write *N* if it is something that a neutral person would have said.

1 _____ "I never thought I would burn my own crops, but it's better than providing food for redcoats."

2 _____ "I don't care who wins; I just want this war to end."

3 _____ "The soldiers have a right to take what they need from people who are nothing but rebels."

4 _____ "I do not understand why my son has chosen to fight on the side of people who betray their king."

5 _____ "People who profiteer are traitors to the cause of freedom."

© Harcourt

CALIFORNIA STANDARDS HSS 5.6, 5.6.4

Skills: Read Parallel Time Lines

DIRECTIONS Use the time lines to answer the questions.

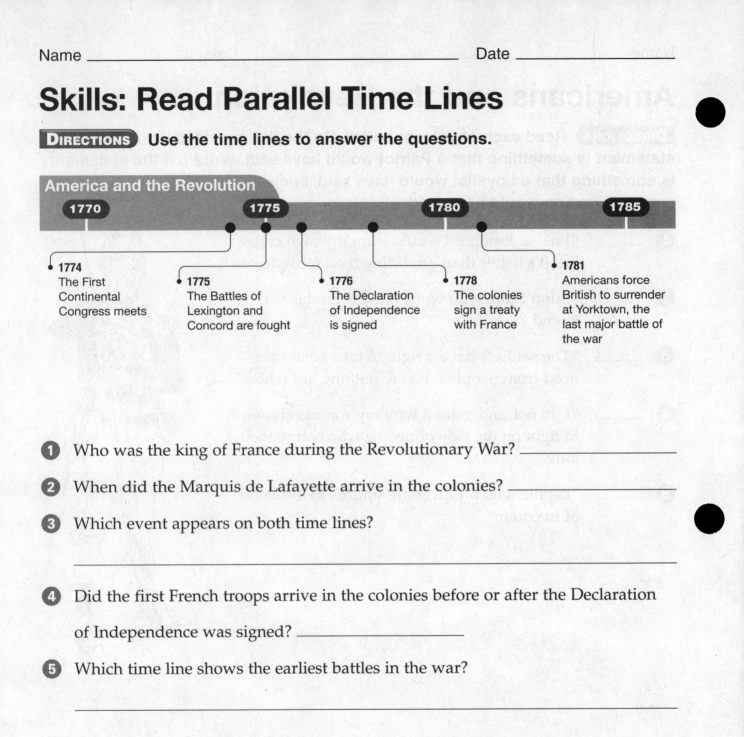

America and the Revolution

1770   1775   1780   1785

1774
The First Continental Congress meets

1775
The Battles of Lexington and Concord are fought

1776
The Declaration of Independence is signed

1778
The colonies sign a treaty with France

1781
Americans force British to surrender at Yorktown, the last major battle of the war

1 Who was the king of France during the Revolutionary War? _____

2 When did the Marquis de Lafayette arrive in the colonies? _____

3 Which event appears on both time lines?

_____

4 Did the first French troops arrive in the colonies before or after the Declaration

of Independence was signed? _____

5 Which time line shows the earliest battles in the war?

_____

CALIFORNIA STANDARDS HSS 5.6, 5.6.2; CS 1   *(continued)*

90 ■ Homework and Practice Book   Use after reading Chapter 9, Skill Lesson, pages 374–375.

© Harcourt

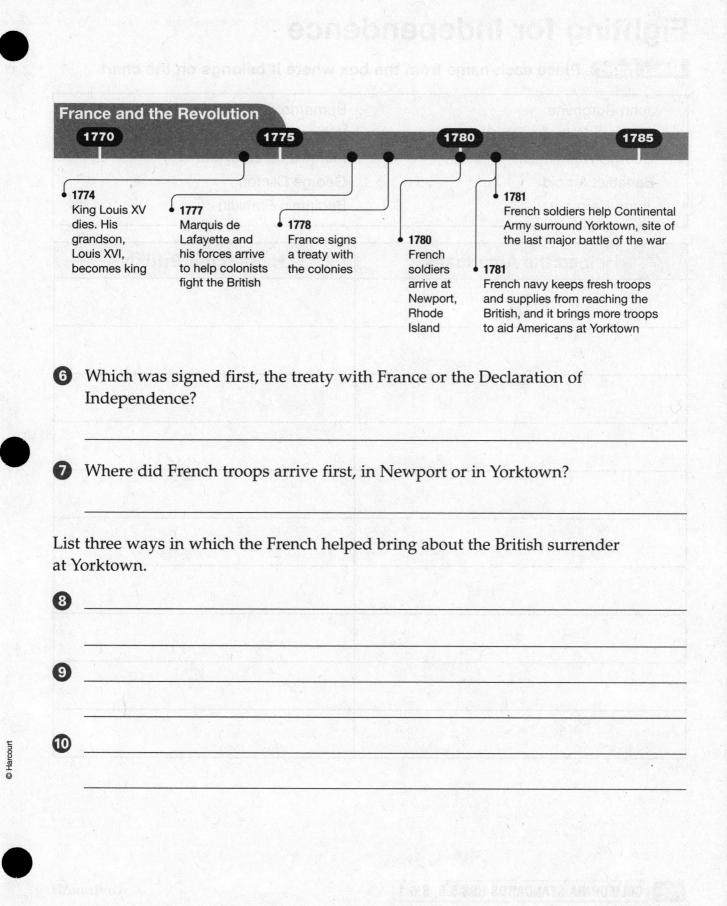

France and the Revolution

1770   1775   1780   1785

1774
King Louis XV dies. His grandson, Louis XVI, becomes king

1777
Marquis de Lafayette and his forces arrive to help colonists fight the British

1778
France signs a treaty with the colonies

1780
French soldiers arrive at Newport, Rhode Island

1781
French soldiers help Continental Army surround Yorktown, site of the last major battle of the war

1781
French navy keeps fresh troops and supplies from reaching the British, and it brings more troops to aid Americans at Yorktown

6 Which was signed first, the treaty with France or the Declaration of Independence?

_____

7 Where did French troops arrive first, in Newport or in Yorktown?

_____

List three ways in which the French helped bring about the British surrender at Yorktown.

8 _____

_____

9 _____

_____

10 _____

_____

© Harcourt

Fighting for Independence

DIRECTIONS Place each name from the box where it belongs on the chart.

John Burgoyne   Bernardo de Gálvez
Friedrich Wilhelm von Steuben   William Howe
George Washington   Marquis de Lafayette
Benedict Arnold   George Clinton
Jorge Farragut   Benjamin Franklin

Helped the Americans	Helped the British

CALIFORNIA STANDARDS HSS 5.6, 5.6.1   *(continued)*

92 ■ Homework and Practice Book   Use after reading Chapter 9, Lesson 2, pages 378–384.

Name _____ Date _____

DIRECTIONS Use phrases from the paragraph below to complete the Venn diagram. Write each phrase in the correct section of the diagram.

The soldiers in both the Continental Army and the British army carried muskets with bayonets into battle, but in other ways these armies were very different. The British army had 50,000 soldiers in the colonies. The soldiers were well trained and experienced in battle. They were also helped by thousands of mercenaries. The Continental Army was made up of less than 15,000 soldiers. Many of these soldiers were farmers who had just signed up for the army. The armies also looked different and carried different things with them. The Continental soldier often wore a tricorn hat and carried a cartridge bag with a sling. The British soldier wore a bright red coat, and carried a haversack for food.

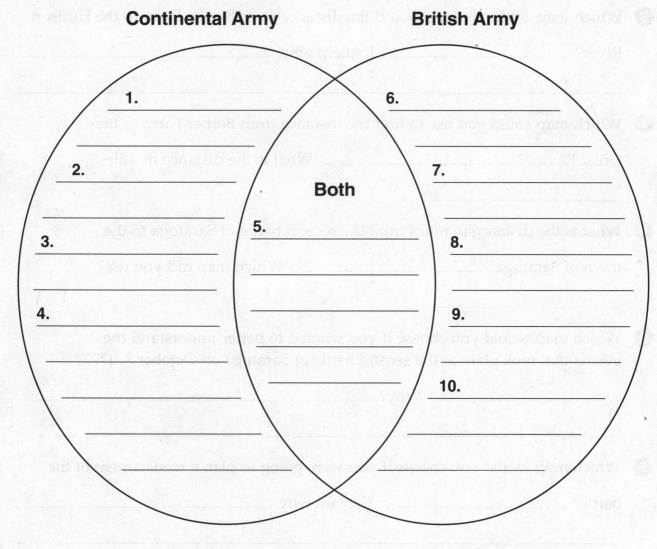

Continental Army   **British Army**

1. _____
_____

2. _____
_____

Both

5. _____
_____

3. _____
_____

4. _____
_____
_____

6. _____
_____

7. _____
_____

8. _____
_____

9. _____

10. _____
_____

Skills: Compare Maps with Different Scales

DIRECTIONS Answer the questions below by choosing the map on page 95 that best answers the question.

1 Which map could you use to find the distance from Saratoga to Albany?

_____

2 Which map could you use to find the distance from Fort Ticonderoga to Saratoga? _____ What is the distance in miles?

_____

3 Which map could you use to find the distance from Barber Farm to the Hudson River? _____ Explain why. _____

_____

4 Which map could you use to find the distance from Barber Farm to the Great Ravine? _____ What is the distance in miles?

_____

5 What is the distance in miles from the second battle of Saratoga to the town of Saratoga? _____ Which map did you use?

_____

6 Which map would you choose if you wanted to better understand the events that took place at the second battle of Saratoga on October 7, 1777? _____ Why? _____

_____

7 Which map would you choose if you were going to plan a reenactment of the battle? _____ Explain why. _____

_____

CALIFORNIA STANDARDS HSS 5.6, 5.6.1; CS 4   *(continued)*

94 ■ **Homework and Practice Book**   Use after reading Chapter 9, Skill Lesson, pages 386–387.

© Harcourt

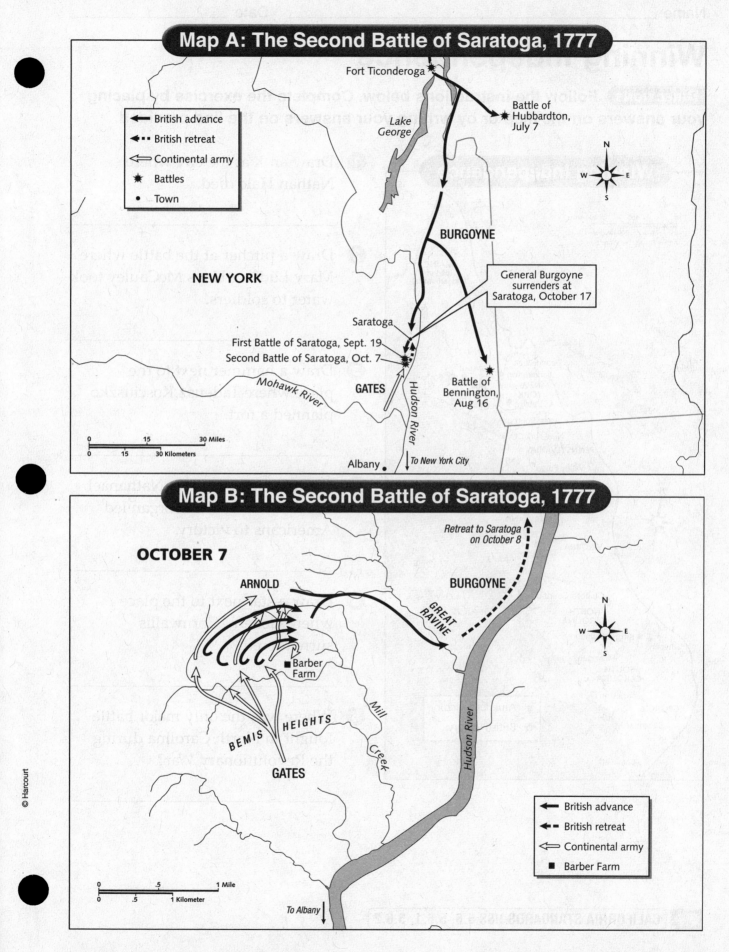

Map A: The Second Battle of Saratoga, 1777

Fort Ticonderoga

Lake George

Battle of Hubbardton, July 7

British advance
British retreat
Continental army
Battles
Town

N
W E
S

BURGOYNE

NEW YORK

General Burgoyne surrenders at Saratoga, October 17

Saratoga

First Battle of Saratoga, Sept. 19
Second Battle of Saratoga, Oct. 7

Mohawk River

GATES

Hudson River

Battle of Bennington, Aug 16

0 15 30 Miles
0 15 30 Kilometers

Albany

↓ To New York City

Map B: The Second Battle of Saratoga, 1777

OCTOBER 7

Retreat to Saratoga on October 8

ARNOLD

BURGOYNE

GREAT RAVINE

Barber Farm

BEMIS HEIGHTS

Mill Creek

Hudson River

GATES

British advance
British retreat
Continental army
Barber Farm

0 .5 1 Mile
0 .5 1 Kilometer

To Albany ↓

Use after reading Chapter 9, Skill Lesson, pages 386–387.

Winning Independence

DIRECTIONS Follow the instructions below. Complete the exercise by placing your answers on the map or by writing your answers on the line provided.

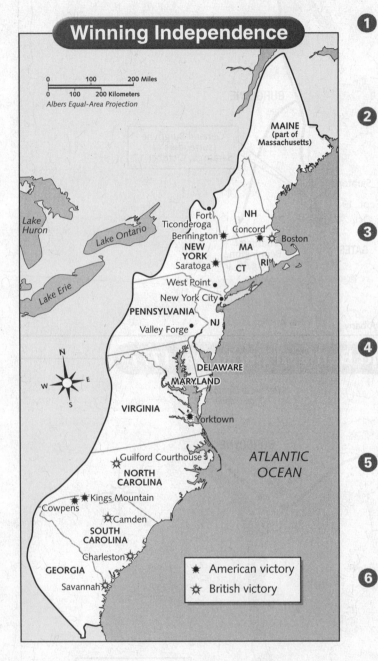

Winning Independence

0   100   200 Miles
0 100 200 Kilometers
Albers Equal-Area Projection

MAINE (part of Massachusetts)

Lake Huron
Lake Ontario
Lake Erie

Fort Ticonderoga
Bennington
NEW YORK
Saratoga
West Point
New York City
PENNSYLVANIA
Valley Forge
NJ

NH
Concord
Boston
MA
CT
RI

DELAWARE
MARYLAND
VIRGINIA
Yorktown

Guilford Courthouse
NORTH CAROLINA
Kings Mountain
Cowpens
Camden
SOUTH CAROLINA
Charleston
GEORGIA
Savannah

ATLANTIC OCEAN

★ American victory
☆ British victory

1 Draw an X at the city where Nathan Hale died.

_____

2 Draw a pitcher at the battle where Mary Ludwig Hays McCauley took water to soldiers.

_____

3 Draw a hammer next to the place where Tadeusz Kosciuszko planned a fort.

_____

4 Circle the place where Nathanael Greene and Daniel Morgan led Americans to victory.

_____

5 Draw a star next to the place where General Cornwallis surrendered.

_____

6 Where was the only major battle fought in North Carolina during the Revolutionary War?

_____

CALIFORNIA STANDARDS HSS 5.6, 5.6.1, 5.6.2

Use after reading Chapter 9, Lesson 3, pages 388–395.

Consequences of the War

DIRECTIONS Read each question and choose the best answer. Then fill in the circle for the answer that you have chosen.

1 Which idea in the Declaration of Independence changed people's views of slavery?

(A) the idea that people must obey the government

(B) the idea that all men have a right to life and liberty

(C) the idea that the colonies would no longer be ruled by Britain

(D) the idea that people should not be taxed without their consent

2 What argument did Elizabeth Freeman use to win her freedom in court?

(A) She argued that all people are born free.

(B) She argued that her owner was cruel.

(C) She argued that slavery had been abolished.

(D) She argued that she had a right to vote.

3 Which state was the first to abolish slavery?

(A) Georgia

(B) Maryland

(C) Massachusetts

(D) Virginia

4 Who formed the nation's first abolitionist group?

(A) slaves

(B) Indians

(C) planters

(D) Quakers

5 What did the Northwest Ordinance say about slavery?

(A) It allowed slavery in the Northwest Territory.

(B) It outlawed slavery in the Northwest Territory.

(C) It said that each state in the Northwest Territory could decide whether to allow slavery.

(D) It did not mention slavery.

CALIFORNIA STANDARDS HSS 5.6, 5.6.6, 5.6.7

Study Guide

DIRECTIONS Fill in the missing information in these paragraphs about the American Revolution. Use the names and terms below to help you complete the paragraphs.

Lesson 1	**Lesson 2**	**Lesson 3**	**Lesson 4**
Sybil Ludington	turning point	Nathan Hale	abolitionists
Thayendanegea	mercenaries	Benedict Arnold	ordinance
Peter Salem	negotiate	John Paul Jones	territories
James Armistead	campaign		
Deborah Sampson			

Lesson 1   The Revolutionary War affected nearly everyone in the colonies.

Women played important roles in the war. A teenager named

_____ warned American troops that the British were

about to attack. _____ disguised herself as a man and

fought in the war. African Americans, too, made important contributions.

_____ won his freedom by working as a spy for George

Washington. _____ and several other African Americans

fought at Concord. American Indian groups allied with both the Americans

and the British. _____ and the Mohawks fought on the side

of the British, while the Oneida and Tuscarora fought for the Americans.

🐻 **CALIFORNIA STANDARDS HSS 5.6, 5.6.1, 5.6.2, 5.6.3, 5.6.5, 5.6.6, 5.6.7**   *(continued)*

98 ▪ Homework and Practice Book   Use after reading Chapter 9, pages 366–401.

© Harcourt

Name _____   Date _____

Lesson 2   In 1777, the British began a _____ to capture

New York. The large British Army was helped by _____

from Germany. Yet the British lost an important battle at Saratoga. This battle

was a _____ in the war. Benjamin Franklin had gone to

France to _____ with French leaders. He wanted France

to help Americans in the war. The American victory at Saratoga convinced

French leaders that colonists could win the war, and they agreed to help.

Lesson 3   The American Revolution created many strong leaders, and a few

traitors. _____ was a Patriot spy who was captured by

the British and hanged. Navy commander _____ fought

the British Navy off the coast of Britain. But _____, who

had led his troops to victory at Saratoga, betrayed his country and helped

the British.

Lesson 4   State constitutions that were written after 1776 embodied the

ideals of the American Revolution. The ideals stated in the Declaration of

Independence led some Americans to believe that slavery was wrong. Some

became _____ and spoke out against slavery. Efforts to

end slavery affected _____ outside the states. In 1787, an

_____ governing lands to the northwest outlawed

slavery in the region.

Name _____ Date _____

READING SOCIAL STUDIES: CAUSE AND EFFECT

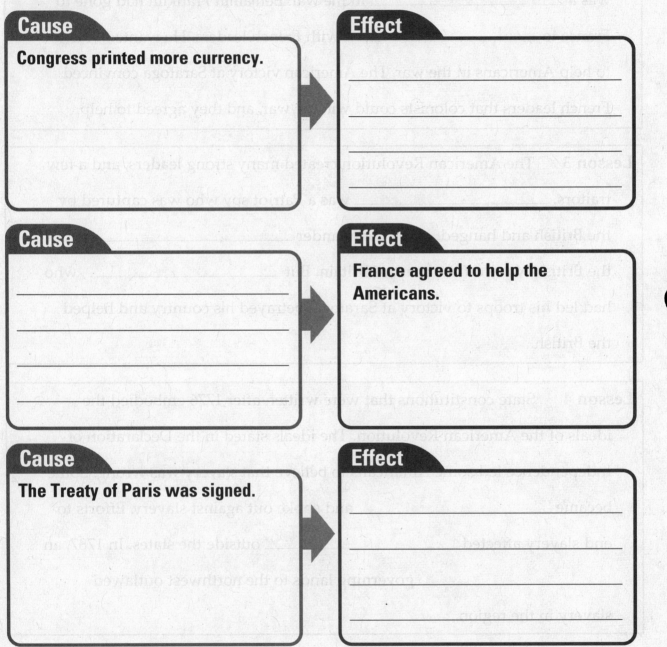

Focus Skill **The Revolutionary War**

DIRECTIONS Complete this graphic organizer to show that you understand the causes and effects of some of the key events of the Revolutionary War.

Cause

Congress printed more currency.

Effect

_____

_____

_____

_____

Cause

_____

_____

_____

_____

Effect

France agreed to help the Americans.

Cause

The Treaty of Paris was signed.

Effect

_____

_____

_____

_____

© Harcourt

![bear] **CALIFORNIA STANDARDS HSS 5.6, 5.6.4**

Name _____ Date _____

The Articles of Confederation

DIRECTIONS Answer the questions below.

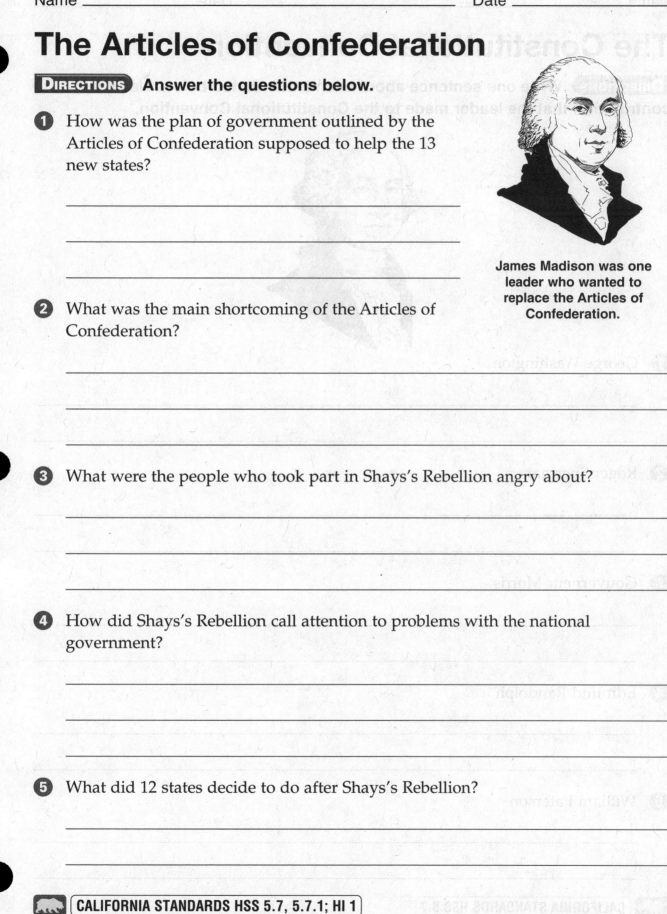

1 How was the plan of government outlined by the Articles of Confederation supposed to help the 13 new states?

_____

_____

_____

James Madison was one leader who wanted to replace the Articles of Confederation.

2 What was the main shortcoming of the Articles of Confederation?

_____

_____

_____

3 What were the people who took part in Shays's Rebellion angry about?

_____

_____

_____

4 How did Shays's Rebellion call attention to problems with the national government?

_____

_____

_____

5 What did 12 states decide to do after Shays's Rebellion?

_____

_____

_____

© Harcourt

CALIFORNIA STANDARDS HSS 5.7, 5.7.1; HI 1

The Constitutional Convention

DIRECTIONS Write one sentence about each leader listed below. Name a contribution that the leader made to the Constitutional Convention.

1 George Washington

_____

_____

2 Roger Sherman

_____

_____

3 Gouverneur Morris

_____

_____

4 Edmund Randolph

_____

_____

5 William Paterson

_____

_____

CALIFORNIA STANDARDS HSS 5.7

Three Branches of Government

DIRECTIONS Use the words and phrases in the box to complete the diagram.

Supreme Court	President	Senate	Executive Branch

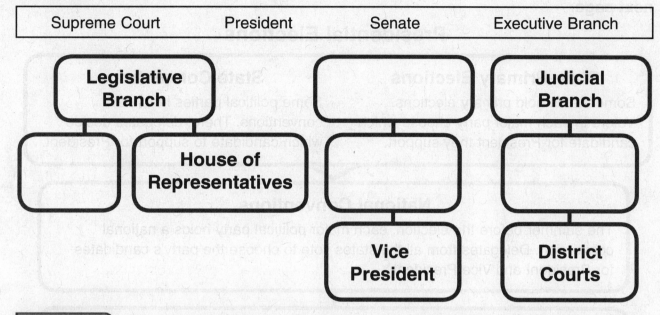

Legislative Branch

House of Representatives

Judicial Branch

Vice President

District Courts

DIRECTIONS Read the list below of positions in the government. In the space provided, write a brief description of the duties of the person holding that job.

1 President

_____

_____

_____

2 Supreme Court justice

_____

_____

_____

3 Representative

_____

_____

_____

© Harcourt

CALIFORNIA STANDARDS HSS 5.7, 5.7.4

Skills: Read a Flowchart

DIRECTIONS Use the flowchart to help you answer the questions on the next page.

Presidential Elections

State Primary Elections

Some states hold primary elections. Voters in each major party choose which candidate for President they support.

State Conventions

Some political parties hold state conventions. There, delegates decide which candidate to support for President.

National Conventions

The summer before the election, each major political party holds a national convention. Delegates from all the states vote to choose the party's candidates for President and Vice President.

Election Day

On the first Tuesday after the first Monday in November, voters cast their ballots. This is called the popular vote.

Electoral Vote

In December, electors meet in each state to pledge their votes for the candidate who won the popular vote. They almost always vote for the candidate who won the popular vote, but they are not required to do so. The electors send the results of their vote to the president of the Senate.

Electoral Count

The president of the Senate counts the electoral votes from all states and announces the winner of the election.

Inauguration

The newly elected President and Vice President take office in a ceremony held on January 20.

© Harcourt

CALIFORNIA STANDARDS HSS 5.7, 5.7.3

(continued)

Name _____ Date _____

1 What step comes before Election Day?

_____

2 Does the electoral vote happen before or after the popular vote?

_____

3 What is the last step in a presidential election?

_____

4 Who counts the electoral votes?

_____

5 Which two parts of the process happen before the national conventions?

_____

©PETER BONO

© Harcourt

Approval and the Bill of Rights

DIRECTIONS Complete the diagram to show the freedoms guaranteed by the
First Amendment.

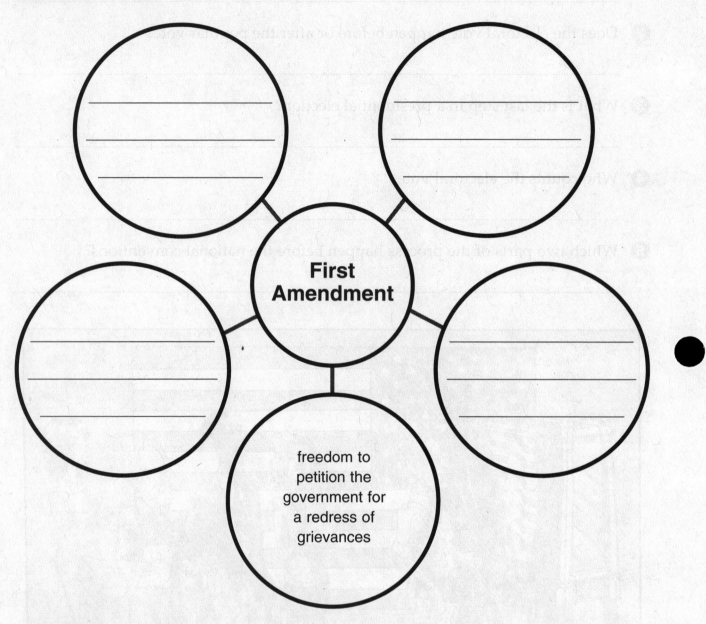

**First
Amendment**

freedom to
petition the
government for
a redress of
grievances

DIRECTIONS Write a sentence telling one way in which people today express
one of these freedoms.

_____

_____

© Harcourt

CALIFORNIA STANDARDS HSS 5.7, 5.7.4   *(continued)*

DIRECTIONS **Next to each number, write the letter of the correct description.**

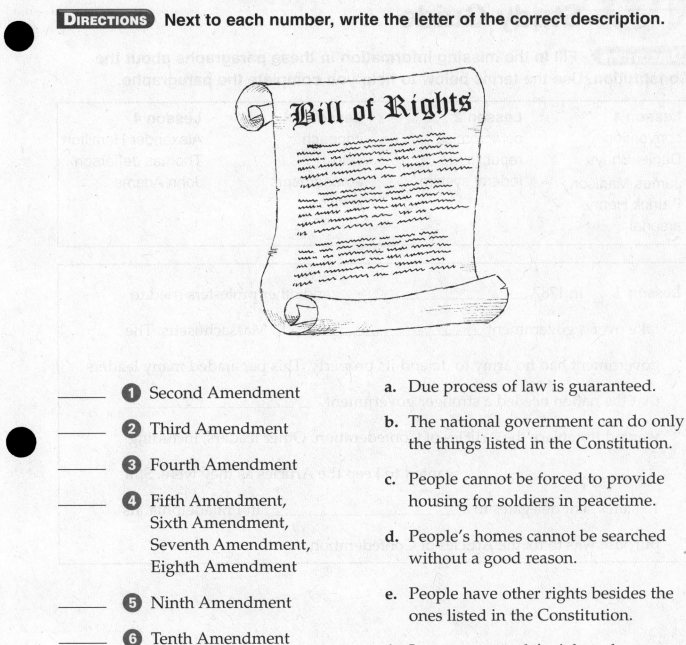

_____ **1** Second Amendment

_____ **2** Third Amendment

_____ **3** Fourth Amendment

_____ **4** Fifth Amendment,
Sixth Amendment,
Seventh Amendment,
Eighth Amendment

_____ **5** Ninth Amendment

_____ **6** Tenth Amendment

a. Due process of law is guaranteed.

b. The national government can do only the things listed in the Constitution.

c. People cannot be forced to provide housing for soldiers in peacetime.

d. People's homes cannot be searched without a good reason.

e. People have other rights besides the ones listed in the Constitution.

f. It protects people's right to have weapons.

Name _____ Date _____

Study Guide

DIRECTIONS Fill in the missing information in these paragraphs about the Constitution. Use the terms below to help you complete the paragraphs.

Lesson 1	**Lesson 2**	**Lesson 3**	**Lesson 4**
convention	compromise	impeach	Alexander Hamilton
Daniel Shays	republic	veto	Thomas Jefferson
James Madison	federal system	amendments	John Adams
Patrick Henry		justices	
arsenal			

Lesson 1   In 1787, _____ and other protesters tried to

take over a government _____ in Massachusetts. The

government had no army to defend its property. This persuaded many leaders

that the nation needed a stronger government. _____

wanted to replace the Articles of Confederation. Other leaders, including

_____ , wanted to keep the Articles as they were. Still,

12 states sent delegates to a _____ in Philadelphia. Its

purpose was to fix the Articles of Confederation.

Name _____ Date _____

Lesson 2   Delegates to the Constitutional Convention had to

_____ to settle their disagreements. Many of these

disagreements were about government powers. The delegates finally agreed

to strengthen the existing _____, in which power

was shared by the national government and the state governments. The

government that the delegates created was a _____, in

which people choose representatives to run the government.

Lesson 3   Under the Constitution, each branch of government limits

the power of the other branches. For example, the President can

_____, or reject, bills that Congress passes. Congress can

_____ the President. The President nominates Supreme

Court _____, but the Senate must approve them. The

Constitution also explains the process for adding _____,

or changes.

Lesson 4   Disagreements among the nation's leaders led to the first political

parties. _____ was a leader of the Federalists, who

wanted a strong federal government. _____ was an

Anti-Federalist who helped form the Democratic-Republican Party. In 1796,

the Federalist candidate, _____, became the nation's

second President.

READING SOCIAL STUDIES: DRAW CONCLUSIONS

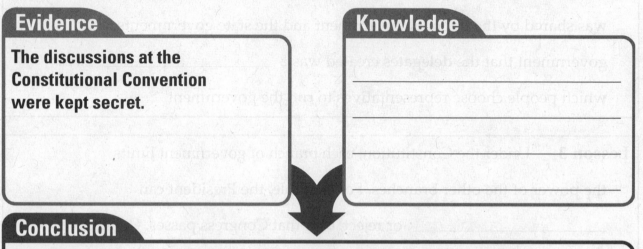

Focus Skill The Constitutional Convention

DIRECTIONS Complete this graphic organizer to show that you can draw conclusions about the Constitutional Convention.

Evidence

The discussions at the Constitutional Convention were kept secret.

Knowledge

_____

_____

_____

_____

Conclusion

The delegates at the Constitutional Convention did not want others to influence their decisions.

Evidence

Delegates who supported the Constitution needed nine states to approve it.

Knowledge

People sometimes have to compromise to get what they want.

Conclusion

_____

_____

© Harcourt

CALIFORNIA STANDARDS HSS 5.7, 5.7.2

A Constitutional Democracy

DIRECTIONS Use the phrases in the box to complete the chart. The arrows show how one branch of the government can affect another.

Heads the armed forces	Approves treaties	Can override the President's veto
Passes taxes	Can rule that a law is unconstitutional	

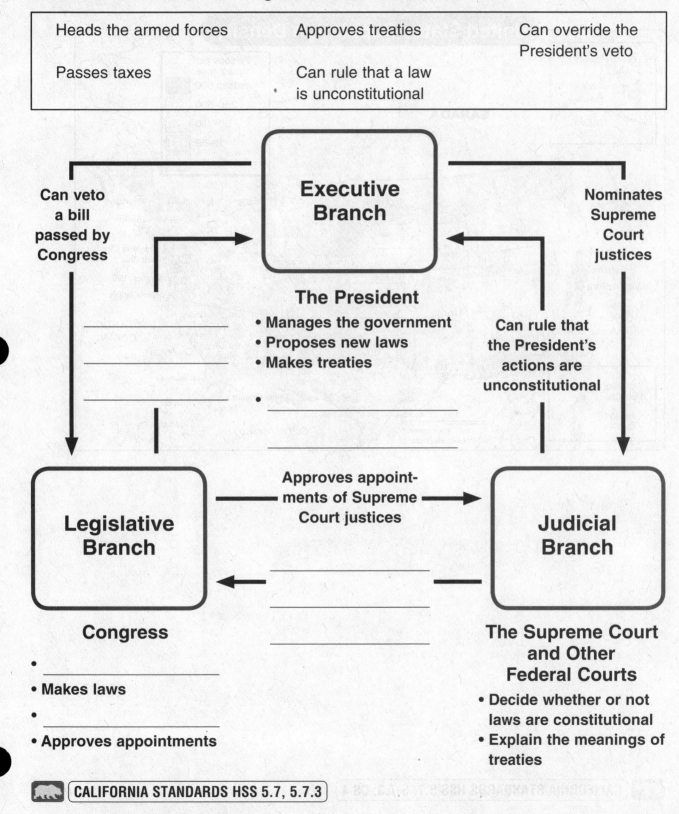

Executive Branch

Can veto a bill passed by Congress

Nominates Supreme Court justices

The President
- Manages the government
- Proposes new laws
- Makes treaties
- _____
- _____

Can rule that the President's actions are unconstitutional

Approves appointments of Supreme Court justices

Legislative Branch

Judicial Branch

_____

Congress
- _____
- Makes laws
- _____
- Approves appointments

The Supreme Court and Other Federal Courts
- Decide whether or not laws are constitutional
- Explain the meanings of treaties

© Harcourt

🐻 **CALIFORNIA STANDARDS HSS 5.7, 5.7.3**

Skills: Read a Population Map

DIRECTIONS Use the map to help you answer the questions.

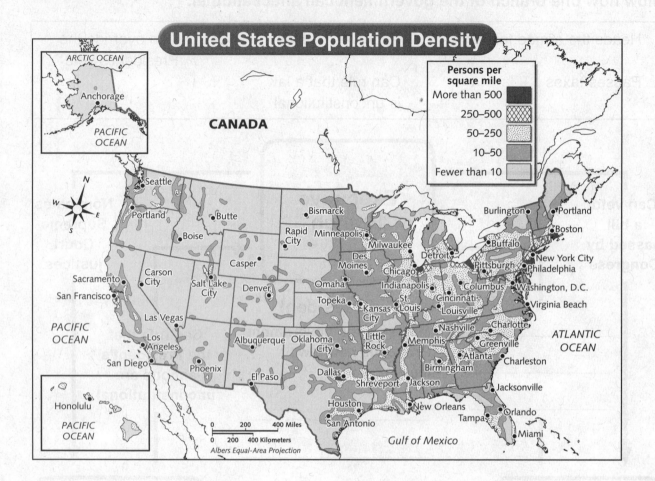

United States Population Density

Persons per square mile
- More than 500
- 250–500
- 50–250
- 10–50
- Fewer than 10

CANADA

ARCTIC OCEAN
Anchorage
PACIFIC OCEAN

Seattle
Portland
Butte
Bismarck
Rapid City
Minneapolis
Milwaukee
Boise
Des Moines
Detroit
Casper
Chicago
Carson City
Salt Lake City
Denver
Omaha
Indianapolis
Columbus
Sacramento
Topeka
St. Louis
Cincinnati
San Francisco
Kansas City
Louisville
Las Vegas
Nashville
Charlotte
Los Angeles
Albuquerque
Oklahoma City
Little Rock
Memphis
Greenville
San Diego
Phoenix
Atlanta
Charleston
El Paso
Dallas
Shreveport
Jackson
Birmingham
Jacksonville
Houston
New Orleans
San Antonio
Orlando
Tampa
Miami
Burlington
Portland
Boston
Buffalo
Pittsburgh
New York City
Philadelphia
Washington, D.C.
Virginia Beach

PACIFIC OCEAN
ATLANTIC OCEAN
Gulf of Mexico

Honolulu
PACIFIC OCEAN

N W E S

0   200   400 Miles
0   200   400 Kilometers
Albers Equal-Area Projection

CALIFORNIA STANDARDS HSS 5.7, 5.7.3; CS 4

(*continued*)

112 ▪ **Homework and Practice Book**   Use after reading Chapter 11, Skill Lesson, pages 464–465.

© Harcourt

Name _____ Date _____

1 Which is more densely populated, the area around Burlington or the area around

Charlotte? _____

2 What is the population density of the area in which Virginia Beach is located?

_____

3 What is the population density in the United States of most of the area bordering
Mexico?

_____

4 What are the most densely populated parts of California?

_____

_____

5 Which part of the country has the higher population density, the East or the

West? _____

6 Which region of the country has the higher population density, the Great Lakes
region or the Pacific Northwest region?

_____

7 Which state has the lowest population density? _____

8 What is the population density where you live? _____
Place an "X" on the map to mark the location.

9 What is the population density of the area surrounding where you live?

_____ Place a circle around the "X" to mark this area.

© Harcourt

Name _____   Date _____

American Ideals

DIRECTIONS Read the following verse of "America the Beautiful." Then answer the questions.

"America the Beautiful"
by Katharine Lee Bates

O, beautiful for spacious skies,
For amber waves of grain,
For purple mountain majesties
Above the fruited plain!
America! America!
God shed his grace on thee,
And crown thy good with brotherhood,
From sea to shining sea!

1 What landforms does the song mention? _____

2 What do the phrases "waves of grain" and "the fruited plain" tell you about America, besides that it is beautiful?

_____

3 What does the phrase "from sea to shining sea" refer to? _____

_____

4 What is one American ideal that the song reflects? _____

_____

5 Write a sentence telling how you feel or what you think of when you read the

words to this song. _____

_____

 **CALIFORNIA STANDARDS HSS 5.7, 5.7.6**

Skills: Read an Editorial Cartoon

DIRECTIONS Read the paragraph below, and then look carefully at the editorial cartoon. Read the labels. Then answer the questions.

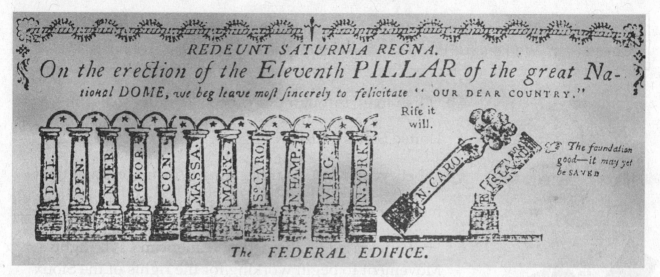

This cartoon uses pillars, or columns, to represent the states involved in building the federal system of government. Those pillars that stand side by side represent states that have already agreed to ratify the Constitution. The last two pillars represent North Carolina and Rhode Island.

1 What do the pillars in the cartoon represent? _____

2 What could the pillars standing together be a symbol of? _____

3 Why are the last two pillars leaning? _____

_____

_____

4 What were the last two states to ratify the Constitution?

_____

_____

5 What does the cartoon express about the federal system?

_____

_____

CALIFORNIA STANDARDS HSS 5.7, 5.7.2

Preserving the Constitution

DIRECTIONS Read the statements below. Then choose the term from the box that best relates to each statement below.

Americans with Disabilities Act (ADA)	American Indian Movement (AIM)
United Farm Workers (UFW)	naturalization civil rights

1 "I had to go through this process in order to become a United States Citizen." _____

2 "I believe in Martin Luther King's dream of equal treatment for all citizens under the law." _____

3 "I was inspired by the African American Civil Rights Movement to begin working for the rights of the Sioux people." _____

4 "My parents worked for grape growers in California for low pay until Cesar Chavez and others organized a boycott to gain better wages." _____

5 "This law makes it easier for me to get a job based on my ability to perform the job." _____

DIRECTIONS Choose an American leader who has worked to uphold the Constitution, and briefly describe his or her contribution to the country.

_____

_____

_____

_____

CALIFORNIA STANDARDS HSS 5.7, 5.7.5

Skills: Act as a Responsible Citizen

DIRECTIONS Read each statement below. Then suggest how you might act as a responsible citizen to handle the situation.

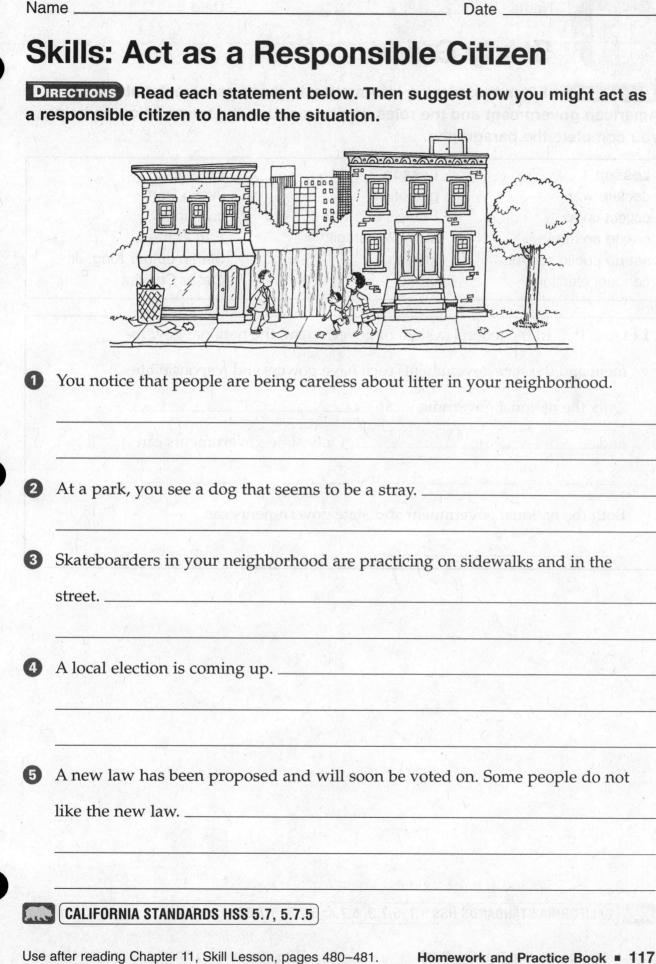

1 You notice that people are being careless about litter in your neighborhood.

_____

_____

2 At a park, you see a dog that seems to be a stray. _____

_____

3 Skateboarders in your neighborhood are practicing on sidewalks and in the

street. _____

_____

4 A local election is coming up. _____

_____

_____

5 A new law has been proposed and will soon be voted on. Some people do not

like the new law. _____

_____

_____

CALIFORNIA STANDARDS HSS 5.7, 5.7.5

© Harcourt

Name _____ Date _____

Study Guide

DIRECTIONS Fill in the missing information in these paragraphs about the American government and the roles of citizens. Use the terms below to help you complete the paragraphs.

Lesson 1	**Lesson 2**	**Lesson 3**
declare war	patriotism	Justin Dart
collect taxes	Francis Scott Key	civil rights
create an army	Mary Pickersgill	Earl Warren
set up public schools	ideals	Martin Luther King, Jr.
conduct elections	creed	Cesar Chavez

Lesson 1   In the federal system of government, the national govern-

ment and the state governments each have powers and responsibilities.

Only the national government can _____

and _____ . Only state governments can

_____ and _____ .

Both the national government and state governments can

_____ .

🐻 **CALIFORNIA STANDARDS HSS 5.7, 5.7.3, 5.7.4, 5.7.5, 5.7.6**   *(continued)*

Name _____ Date _____

Lesson 2   The principles of freedom, equality, and justice are at the

heart of the American _____, or system of beliefs.

These principles are _____, or goals,

that Americans work to put into practice. Some well-known symbols

and songs are reminders of these goals. One important national symbol

is the American flag. _____ made the flag that

inspired what later became the national anthem. Our national anthem,

"The Star-Spangled Banner," is a song of _____.

It was written by _____ .

Lesson 3   Many Americans have worked to make sure that the

_____ of all Americans are protected.

_____, showed African Americans how to

use nonviolent means to win their rights. Under former Chief Justice

_____, the Supreme Court made decisions that

upheld these rights. _____ worked to improve the

lives of migrant farm workers. _____ helped get a

law passed that protects the rights of disabled persons.

Name _____ Date _____

READING SOCIAL STUDIES: DRAW CONCLUSIONS
⭐ Focus Skill Working for Equality

DIRECTIONS Complete this graphic organizer to show that you can draw conclusions about how people worked to preserve American ideals.

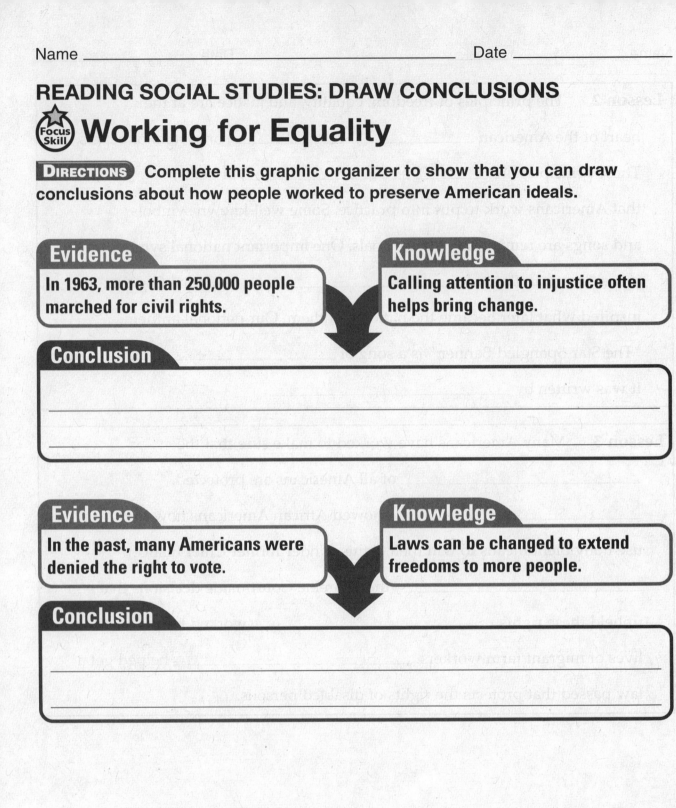

Evidence

In 1963, more than 250,000 people marched for civil rights.

Knowledge

Calling attention to injustice often helps bring change.

Conclusion

_____

_____

Evidence

In the past, many Americans were denied the right to vote.

Knowledge

Laws can be changed to extend freedoms to more people.

Conclusion

_____

_____

 **CALIFORNIA STANDARDS HSS 5.7, 5.7.5**

A Growing Population

DIRECTIONS Use the map to help you answer the questions.

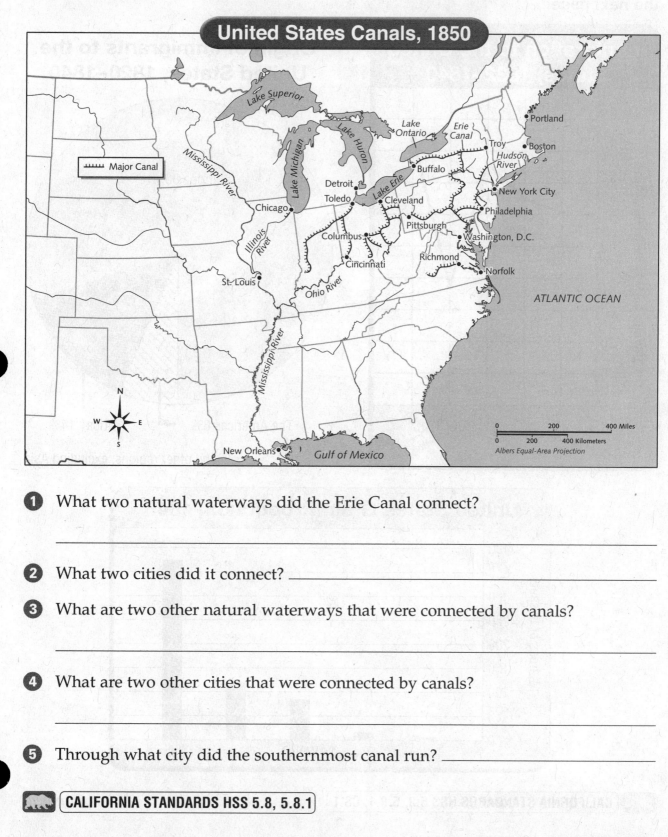

United States Canals, 1850

1 What two natural waterways did the Erie Canal connect?

_____

2 What two cities did it connect? _____

3 What are two other natural waterways that were connected by canals?

_____

4 What are two other cities that were connected by canals?

_____

5 Through what city did the southernmost canal run? _____

CALIFORNIA STANDARDS HSS 5.8, 5.8.1

Skills: Compare Graphs

DIRECTIONS Compare the graphs below to help you answer the questions on the next page.

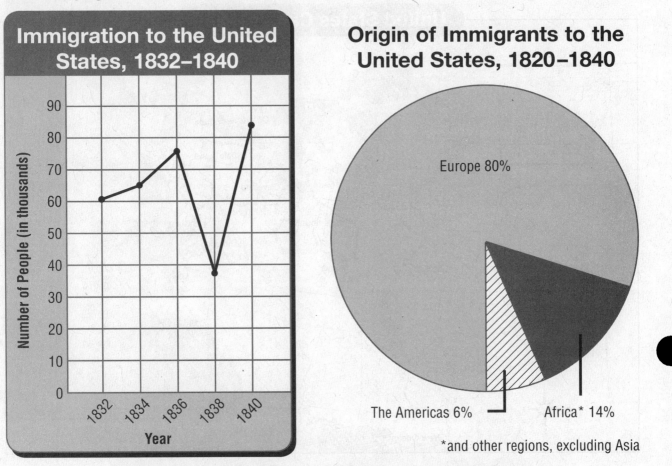

Immigration to the United States, 1832–1840

Number of People (in thousands): 90, 80, 70, 60, 50, 40, 30, 20, 10, 0

Year: 1832, 1834, 1836, 1838, 1840

Origin of Immigrants to the United States, 1820–1840

Europe 80%

The Americas 6%   Africa* 14%

*and other regions, excluding Asia

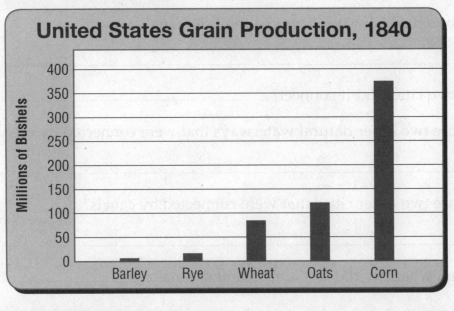

United States Grain Production, 1840

Millions of Bushels: 400, 350, 300, 250, 200, 150, 100, 50, 0

Barley, Rye, Wheat, Oats, Corn

CALIFORNIA STANDARDS HSS 5.8, 5.8.1; CS 1

(continued)

A Growing Nation

DIRECTIONS Use the time line to help you answer the questions below.

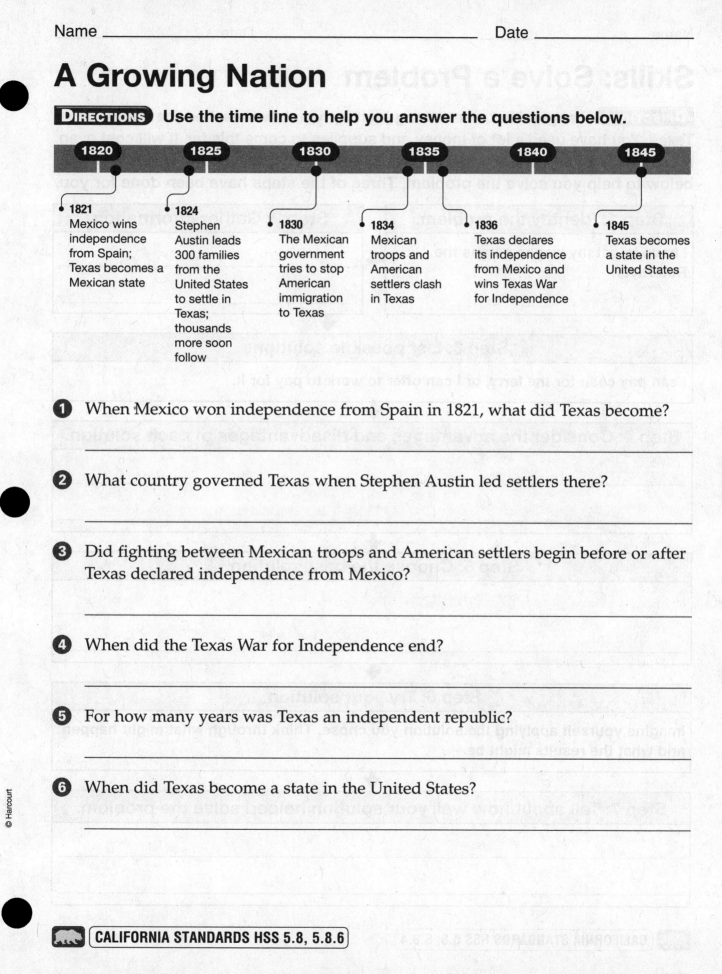

| 1820 | 1825 | 1830 | 1835 | 1840 | 1845 |

1821
Mexico wins independence from Spain; Texas becomes a Mexican state

1824
Stephen Austin leads 300 families from the United States to settle in Texas; thousands more soon follow

1830
The Mexican government tries to stop American immigration to Texas

1834
Mexican troops and American settlers clash in Texas

1836
Texas declares its independence from Mexico and wins Texas War for Independence

1845
Texas becomes a state in the United States

1 When Mexico won independence from Spain in 1821, what did Texas become?

_____

2 What country governed Texas when Stephen Austin led settlers there?

_____

3 Did fighting between Mexican troops and American settlers begin before or after Texas declared independence from Mexico?

_____

4 When did the Texas War for Independence end?

_____

5 For how many years was Texas an independent republic?

_____

6 When did Texas become a state in the United States?

_____

© Harcourt

CALIFORNIA STANDARDS HSS 5.8, 5.8.6

Skills: Solve a Problem

DIRECTIONS Imagine that, after a long journey, you have reached the border of Texas. You have used a lot of money and supplies to come this far. It will cost even more to have your wagon ferried across the Red River to Texas. Use the steps below to help you solve the problem. Three of the steps have been done for you.

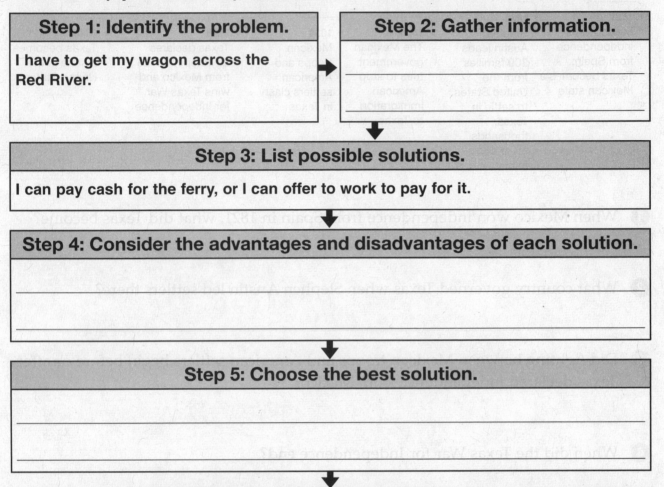

Step 1: Identify the problem.

I have to get my wagon across the Red River.

Step 2: Gather information.

_____

_____

_____

Step 3: List possible solutions.

I can pay cash for the ferry, or I can offer to work to pay for it.

Step 4: Consider the advantages and disadvantages of each solution.

_____

_____

Step 5: Choose the best solution.

_____

_____

Step 6: Try your solution.

Imagine yourself applying the solution you chose. Think through what might happen and what the results might be.

Step 7: Tell about how well your solution helped solve the problem.

_____

_____

🐻 **CALIFORNIA STANDARDS HSS 5.8, 5.8.4**

© Harcourt

Name _____ Date _____

From Ocean to Ocean

DIRECTIONS Next to each name of each person, write the letter of the description that tells about that person.

1 _____ James K. Polk

a. arranged for the United States to buy land from Mexico

2 _____ Mariano Vallejo

b. owned the land where gold was first discovered in California

3 _____ John Sutter

c. worked for California statehood

4 _____ James Buchanan

d. expanded United States territory both to the north and to the south

5 _____ Zachary Taylor

e. signed the bill making Oregon a state

6 _____ James Gadsden

f. gave orders to have a fort built on land Mexico had claimed

DIRECTIONS Imagine that you have been asked to write an interview for a local newspaper. On a separate sheet of paper, write three questions that you would ask during an interview with one of the individuals listed above.

© Harcourt

CALIFORNIA STANDARDS HSS 5.8, 5.8.6

Skills: Identify Changing Borders

DIRECTIONS Use the map to help you answer the questions.

The Growth of the United States

RUSSIA ALASKA PURCHASE 1867 CANADA

PACIFIC OCEAN

Present-day border

OREGON TERRITORY 1846

TREATY WITH BRITAIN 1818

TREATY WITH BRITAIN 1842

MEXICAN CESSION 1848

LOUISIANA PURCHASE 1803

UNITED STATES 1783

PACIFIC OCEAN

GADSDEN PURCHASE 1853

TEXAS ANNEXATION 1845

1810

1812 1813

FLORIDA 1819

ATLANTIC OCEAN

HAWAII ANNEXATION 1898

PACIFIC OCEAN

Gulf of Mexico

1. In what year did the United States add the most new territory? _____

2. What was the last territory added to the United States? _____

3. What present-day state became part of the United States in 1845?

_____

4. In what year did California become part of the United States? _____

5. What generalization can you make about the direction of the growth of the

United States? _____

CALIFORNIA STANDARDS HSS 5.8, 5.8.2, 5.8.6; CS 4

Notes

Notes

Notes

Notes

Notes